# More Bible Activities
# You Can Do

# More Bible Activities You Can Do

**Nell deVries and Mary Currier**

Illustrated by Cheryl Strikwerda Randall

**BakerBooks**
A Division of Baker Book House Co
Grand Rapids, Michigan 49516

© 1999 by Nell deVries and Mary Currier

Published by Baker Books
a division of Baker Book House Company
P.O. Box 6287, Grand Rapids, MI 49516-6287

Taken from *Ready-to-Use Bible Activity Sheets* by Nellie deVries (1992) and *You-Can-Do Bible Activity Sheets* by Mary Currier (1990)

ISBN 0-8010-4416-2

Printed in the United States of America

Unless otherwise indicated Scripture quotations are taken from the King James Version of the Bible. Other versions cited are the New International Version (NIV) and the New King James Version (NKJV).

For current information about all releases from Baker Book House, visit our web site:
http://www.bakerbooks.com

# Contents

# Old Testament

# 1. Creation

Find as many words as you can in the letters below. Go from left to right. The first one is done for you.

**(GOD)DAYSEEDENSEASONSFOWLAIRBEAST**

1. _____GOD_____

2. _____

3. _____

4. _____

5. _____

6. _____

7. _____

8. _____

9. _____

10. _____

11. _____

12. _____

13. _____

14. _____

15. _____

16. _____

17. _____

18. _____

19. _____

20. _____

**Super Word Finder!**

21. _____

22. _____

23. _____

24. _____

25. _____

# 2. The Garden of Eden

Use the code to find the names of two special trees in the Garden of Eden.

Which tree did God tell Adam and Eve not to eat from?

# 3. Noah's Ark

Noah built an ark of gopher wood (Gen. 6:14).

Up, down, across, or diagonally—how many times can you find the word "ARK"?

```
A R K A R K K R A A
A K A R R R K A R A
R A R K A A R K A R
A K A R A R K K A R K A
A R R R A R R K K R A K R R K K
K A K R K A R K R R A K A A A R
R R R K A A K R A R R R R K
A K A A K R A K K A K R
R R R R K R A K R R
K R A R K R A A
```

# 4. Lot's Choice

Abraham and Lot had many animals. There wasn't enough grass for both of their herds, so they decided to part. Abraham said, "If you go to the left, I'll go to the right." Lot saw that the plain of the Jordan was well watered.

Use the code to find out what Lot chose.

Was Lot's choice a good one?

# 5. Abraham and Isaac Worship on the Mountain

God told Abraham to go to a mountain and offer his son Isaac as a sacrifice. Abraham obeyed, but God stopped him from hurting Isaac. Follow the maze up the mountain to find out why Isaac wasn't sacrificed.

\_\_\_ \_\_\_\_, "\_\_\_\_ \_ \_\_\_\_\_

\_\_\_\_ \_\_\_ \_\_\_\_ \_\_\_."

\_\_\_ \_\_\_\_\_ \_\_\_\_

_____ \_\_\_ \_\_\_\_.

# 6. Stairway to Heaven

## Genesis 28

Add or subtract the number of letters written under each line.

| A B C D E F G H I J K L M N O P Q R S T U V W X Y Z |
|---|

Jacob went on a  J  ___ ___ ___ ___ ___ ___  to visit
          L-2   M+2   V-1   S-1   L+2   D+1   Z-1

relatives. He was ___ ___ ___ ___ ___ so he lay down on
          Q+3   J-1   S-1   C+2   F-2

the ground. He used a ___ ___ ___ ___ ___ for a pillow.
          T-1   W-3   L+3   Q-3   B+3

That night Jacob had a beautiful ___ ___ ___ ___ ___.
          F-2   P+2   A+4   C-2   L+1

He saw a stairway leading to heaven with

___ ___ ___ ___ ___ ___ on it. ___ ___ ___ was at the
D-3   L+2   H-1   G-2   K+1   R+1       F+1   R-3   E-1

top and spoke to Jacob. God ___ ___ ___ ___ ___ ___ ___
          A+1   M-1   G-2   U-2   V-3   B+3   F-2

him and promised to be with Jacob.

When Jacob woke up he poured ___ ___ ___ on the stone and
          N+1   J-1   K+1

made a ___ ___ ___ ___ ___ ___ ___ to God. Jacob called the
      S-3   Q+1   N+1   N-1   G+2   U-2   H-3

place ___ ___ ___ ___ ___ ___, which means "The House of
     E-3   C+2   V-2   J-2   C+2   K+1

God."

# 7. Sons of Jacob

Jacob had twelve sons. Fit their names in the stack-a-word puzzle below.

REUBEN
SIMEON
LEVI
JUDAH
DAN
NAPHTALI
GAD
ASHER
ISSACHAR
ZEBULUN
JOSEPH
BENJAMIN

# 8. Wilderness Menu

## Exodus 16

The Israelites needed food while they traveled to Canaan. God sent manna.

Look up the verses in your Bible to find some manna facts. Write the answers on the lines below.

1. How much manna was each person to gather? (v. 16)

2. How long did the Israelites eat manna? (v. 35)

3. What did God call the manna? (v. 4)

4. What did manna taste like? (v. 31)

5. What else did the Israelites get to eat every day? (v. 13)

1. _ _ M _ _ _

2. _ _ _ _ _ _ _ _ _ A _ _

3. _ _ _ _ _ _ _ _ _ _ _ _ _ _ _ _ N

4. _ _ _ N _ _

5. _ _ _ A _ _

# 9. The Golden Calf

God gave Moses the Ten Commandments on Mount Sinai. Moses was on the mountain a long time, and the people became impatient.

The people asked Aaron to make an idol. Aaron used the people's gold jewelry to make a golden calf.

The people worshiped the calf. When Moses came down and saw what was happening, he became very angry.

To find out what Moses did, solve the puzzles.

Take the letters in each column and put them in the same order in the squares above the column. A black square marks the end of a word.

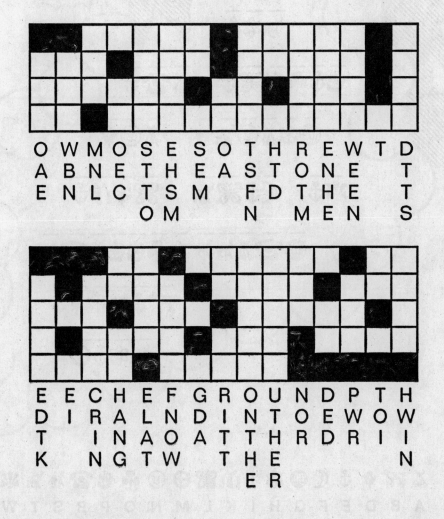

```
O W M O S E S O T H R E W T D
A B N E T H E A S T O N E   T T
E N L C T S M   F D T H E   T S
    O M       N   M E N       S
```

```
E E C H E F G R O U N D P T H
D I R A L N D I N T O E W O W
T   I N A O A T T H R D R I   I
K   N G T W   T H E           N
                E R
```

# 10. The Cluster of Grapes

## Numbers 13

Moses sent twelve men to spy on the land of Canaan. They were to find out what kind of land it was, what fruit and other crops grew in it, and what kind of people were living in it.

The spies found a cluster of grapes so big that two men had to carry it on a pole between them.

Use the code to find out what the spies said about the people of Canaan.

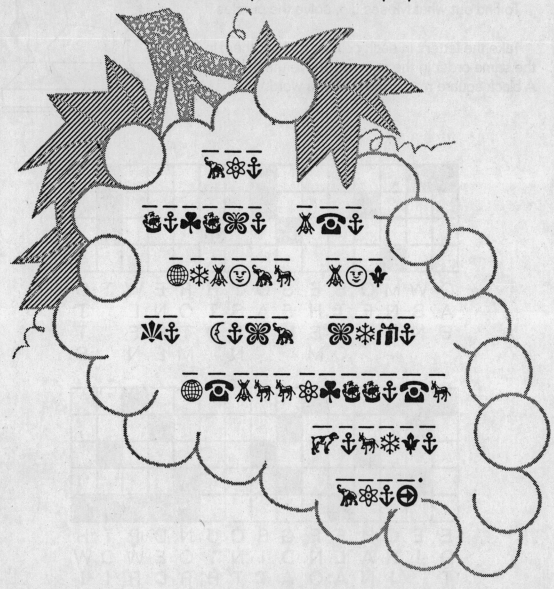

ABDEFGHIKLMNOPRSTW

# 11. A Talking Donkey

Balak, the king of Moab, was afraid because the Israelites had been winning many battles and now were ready to enter the land of Moab. King Balak offered a lot of money to Balaam, a man of God, if he would come and curse the Israelites.

Balaam rode his donkey to visit the king. On his way, the donkey stopped. It saw an angel with a sword on the road. Balaam hit the donkey but it wouldn't move. Then God allowed the donkey to speak. "Why did you beat me?" asked the donkey. "I have always obeyed you."

Then God opened Balaam's eyes and he saw the angel. Balaam bowed before the angel. The angel said, "The donkey saved your life. I would have killed you."

Balaam said, "I have sinned. I will go back home."

Use the dial-a-message code to find out what the angel told Balaam.

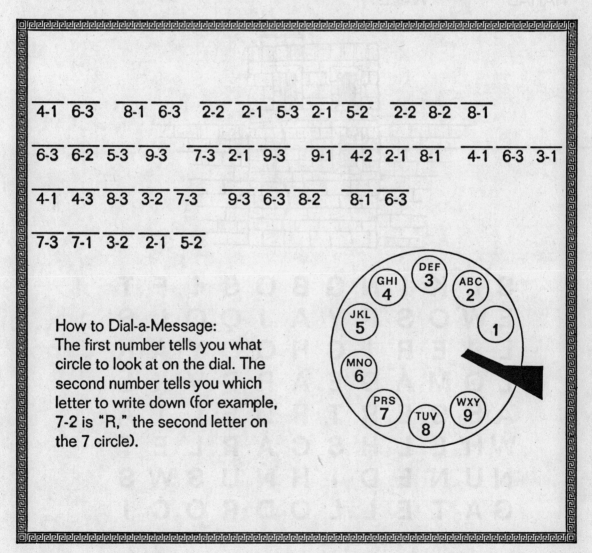

4-1  6-3   8-1  6-3   2-2  2-1  5-3  2-1  5-2   2-2  8-2  8-1

6-3  6-2  5-3  9-3   7-3  2-1  9-3   9-1  4-2  2-1  8-1   4-1  6-3  3-1

4-1  4-3  8-3  3-2  7-3   9-3  6-3  8-2   8-1  6-3

7-3  7-1  3-2  2-1  5-2

How to Dial-a-Message:
The first number tells you what circle to look at on the dial. The second number tells you which letter to write down (for example, 7-2 is "R," the second letter on the 7 circle).

# 12. Rahab

Rahab helped two Israelite spies hide and later escape from her house in Jericho.

The following words were taken from Joshua 2. Find and circle them in the word search.

| | | | |
|---|---|---|---|
| JOSHUA | JORDAN | KING | CORD |
| NUN | SWEAR | ISRAEL | SCARLET |
| SENT | LORD | TWO | OATH |
| SPY | SAVE | GATE | STALKS |
| JERICHO | HIDE | ROOF | FLAX |
| RAHAB | WALL | | |

```
S L K I N G B O S I F T
E W O S P Y A J Q O L S
L J E R I C H O O Y A K
L O M A D E A R P V X L
A S S E R T R D E L I A
W H E L H S C A R L E T
N U N E D I H N U S W S
G A T E L L O D R O C I
```

# 13. The Twelve Tribes of Israel

Each of the twelve tribes lived in a different area in Israel. Write the name of each tribe in the proper location on the map. The code and your Bible map will help you.

x Asher

◊ Benjamin

Ω Dan

□ Ephraim

o Gad

∞ Issachar

Σ Judah

≠ Manasseh

✝ Naphtali

√ Reuben

» Simeon

± Zebulun

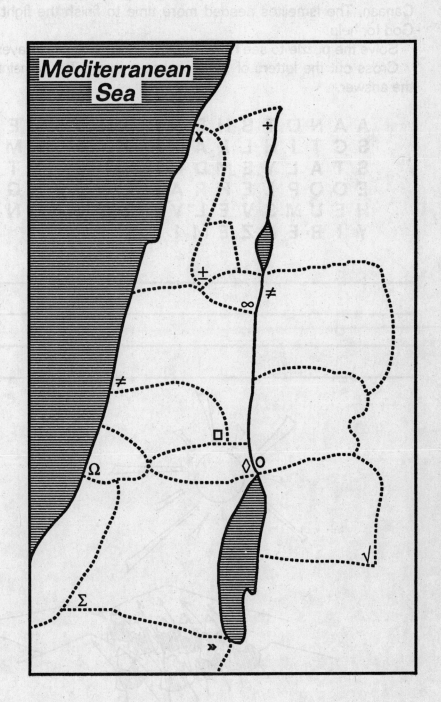

# 14. The Sun Stands Still

## Joshua 10

Joshua and the Israelites were fighting a major battle against five kings of Canaan. The Israelites needed more time to finish the fight. Joshua prayed to God for help.

Solve the puzzle to see how God answered Joshua's prayer.

Cross out the letters of the alphabet in order. The remaining letters spell out the answer.

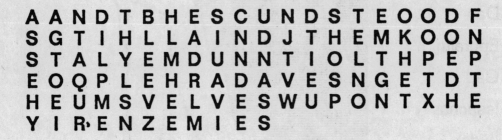

```
A A N D T B H E S C U N D S T E O O D F
S G T I H L L A I N D J T H E M K O O N
S T A L Y E M D U N N T I O L T H P E P
E O Q P L E H R A D A V E S N G E T D T
H E U M S V E L V E S W U P O N T X H E
Y I R E N Z E M I E S
```

_____

_____

_____

_____

# 15. Deborah

The story of Deborah is found in Judges 4 and 5. Deborah is the only female judge mentioned in the Bible. She was also a prophetess.

Deborah helped Barak go to battle against Sisera, the captain of the Canaanite army.

Sisera and his men ran away. Sisera hid in the tent of a woman named Jael. She gave him a drink and let him sleep. Then she killed him.

When Barak came he found Sisera dead.

Judges 5 is the song that Deborah sang about the battle.

Fit the underlined words into the acrostic puzzle.

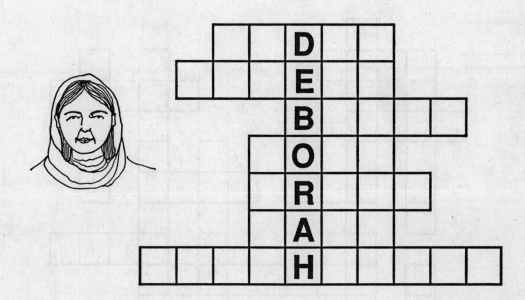

# 16. Gideon

DENS
CAVES
GRASSHOPPERS
OAK
BASKET

ROCK
FIRE
FLEECE
DEW
TENT

BREAD
LAMP
PITCHERS
TRUMPETS
SWORDS

What a strange list of words! See how these words fit together by reading the story of Gideon in Judges 6, 7, and 8. Then fit the words in the puzzle.

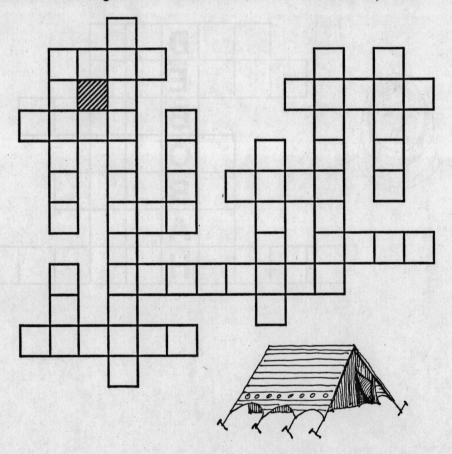

# 17. Ruth

All the words listed below are taken from the Book of Ruth. They can be found horizontally, vertically, or diagonally in the word search.

RUTH
ELIMELECH
NAOMI
MAHLON
CHILION
BETHLEHEM
ORPAH

MOAB
BOAZ
MARA
OBED
JESSE
DAVID
CORN

GLEAN
EPHAH
KIN
REAP
SON
FEET
OLD

```
J  A  C  K  F  B  R  Q  R
E  P  H  A  H  E  O  U  N
S  N  I  K  A  T  T  A  O
S  O  L  P  I  H  E  S  Z
E  L  I  M  E  L  E  C  H
S  H  O  O  G  E  F  O  A
O  A  N  A  O  H  B  R  P
N  M  E  B  L  E  A  N  R
D  A  V  I  D  M  Q  W  O
```

# 18. Samuel

## 1 Samuel 7

Samuel told the people to stop serving idols and to worship only God.

The Philistines came to fight the Israelites, and Samuel prayed to God for help. God sent a great thunderstorm. It frightened the Philistines, and the Israelites chased them away.

Samuel set up a large stone as a symbol to help the Israelites remember the day God helped them.

Write down the first letter of each picture to find the name of the stone.

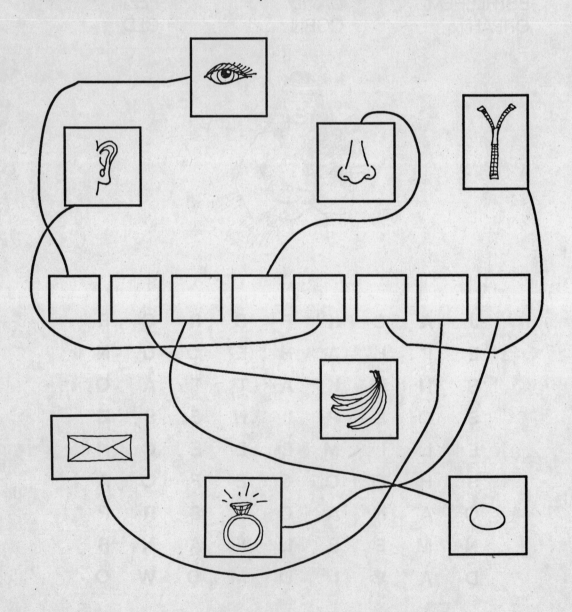

# 19. The First King

Add or subtract the number of letters written under each line.

> A B C D E F G H I J K L M N O P Q R S T U V W X Y Z

The people of __I__ ___ ___ ___ ___ ___ wanted a king.
              J-1  Q+2  O+3  B-1  C+2  M-1

God showed ___ ___ ___ ___ ___ ___ who to pick.
            T-1  C-2  J+3  X-3  C+2  N-2

He was an ___ ___ ___ ___ ___ ___ ___ ___ ___ ,
         E+4  P+3  T-2  B-1  E+0  K+1  K-2  W-3  A+4

of the tribe of ___ ___ ___ ___ ___ ___ ___ ,
            B-0  D+1  P-2  G+3  D-3  K+2  J-1  N+0

of the family of ___ ___ ___ ___ .
             H+3  F+3  W-4  L-4

His name was ___ ___ ___ ___ .
            Z-7  F-5  R+3  M-1

And all the people shouted:

God save the king!

# 20. The Brave Young Prince

Read 1 Samuel 14 to find out why Jonathan, Saul's son, is called a brave young prince.

The following words are taken from 1 Samuel 14. Fit them into the stack-a-word puzzle.

| | | |
|---|---|---|
| ARMOUR | FELL | ROCK |
| DIE | FOOD | ROD |
| DIPPED | GIBEAH | SAUL |
| EAT | GOD | SIN |
| ELI | HONEY | SLAY |
| ENEMIES | ISRAEL | SWORD |
| EPHOD | KISH | TAKEN |
| EYES | LOT | TASTED |
| FAINT | NER | TWENTY |
| FEARED | OATH | YOKE |

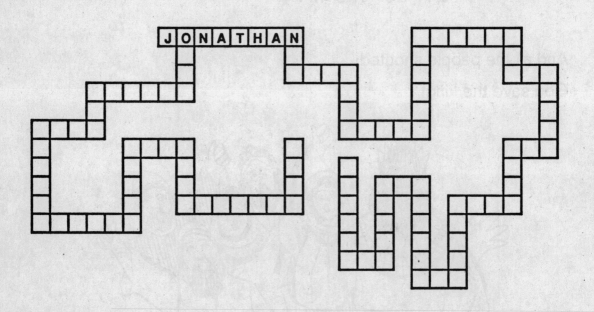

It may be that the LORD will work for us:
for there is no restraint to the LORD
to save us by many or by few.
1 Samuel 14:6b

# 21. The Shepherd Boy of Bethlehem

## 1 Samuel 16

God was not pleased with Saul as king of Israel. God told Samuel to pick another king from the tribe of Judah. Samuel knew that the new king would be one of Jesse's sons. When Samuel thought he had picked a good king, God said, "No." Solve the puzzle to find out how God picks a king.

**M**

$\overline{\text{3-3}}$ $\overline{\text{1-5}}$ $\overline{\text{4-3}}$ $\;\;$ $\overline{\text{2-3}}$ $\overline{\text{5-3}}$ $\overline{\text{5-3}}$ $\overline{\text{1-3}}$ $\overline{\text{4-2}}$ $\;\;$ $\overline{\text{1-5}}$ $\overline{\text{5-2}}$ $\;\;$ $\overline{\text{5-2}}$ $\overline{\text{3-4}}$ $\overline{\text{5-5}}$

$\overline{\text{5-3}}$ $\overline{\text{1-1}}$ $\overline{\text{5-2}}$ $\overline{\text{3-1}}$ $\overline{\text{1-5}}$ $\overline{\text{3-2}}$ $\overline{\text{4-5}}$

$\overline{\text{1-5}}$ $\overline{\text{1-2}}$ $\overline{\text{1-2}}$ $\overline{\text{5-5}}$ $\overline{\text{1-5}}$ $\overline{\text{3-2}}$ $\overline{\text{1-5}}$ $\overline{\text{4-3}}$ $\overline{\text{3-5}}$ $\overline{\text{5-5}}$ $\;\;$ $\overline{\text{2-5}}$ $\overline{\text{1-1}}$ $\overline{\text{5-2}}$

$\overline{\text{5-2}}$ $\overline{\text{3-4}}$ $\overline{\text{5-5}}$ $\;\;$ $\overline{\text{2-3}}$ $\overline{\text{5-3}}$ $\overline{\text{3-2}}$ $\overline{\text{4-5}}$ $\;\;$ $\overline{\text{2-3}}$ $\overline{\text{5-3}}$ $\overline{\text{5-3}}$ $\overline{\text{1-3}}$ $\overline{\text{4-2}}$

$\overline{\text{1-5}}$ $\overline{\text{5-2}}$ $\;\;$ $\overline{\text{5-2}}$ $\overline{\text{3-4}}$ $\overline{\text{5-5}}$ $\;\;$ $\overline{\text{3-4}}$ $\overline{\text{5-5}}$ $\overline{\text{1-5}}$ $\overline{\text{3-2}}$ $\overline{\text{5-2}}$

| | | | | |
|---|---|---|---|---|
| **5** | A | B | C | D | E |
| **4** | F | G | H | I | J |
| **3** | K | L | M | N | O |
| **2** | P | Q | R | S | T |
| **1** | U | V | W | X | Y |
| | **1** | **2** | **3** | **4** | **5** |

To find the correct letter in the graph go across the bottom line till you get to the first number in the code (3-2). The second number indicates the number of rows you need to go up (3-2). (3-2) is the letter "R."

Which son did God tell Samuel to anoint as king?

$\overline{\text{4-5}}$ $\overline{\text{1-5}}$ $\overline{\text{2-1}}$ $\overline{\text{4-4}}$ $\overline{\text{4-5}}$

# 22. David and Goliath

Find as many words as you can in the letters below. Go from left to right. The first one is done for you.

(SWORD)STONESTENTSLINGODOGIANT

1. __SWORD__

2. _____

3. _____

4. _____

5. _____

6. _____

7. _____

8. _____

9. _____

10. _____

11. _____

12. _____

13. _____

14. _____

15. _____

16. _____

17. _____

18. _____

19. _____

20. _____

**Super Word Finder!**

21. _____

22. _____

23. _____

24. _____

25. _____

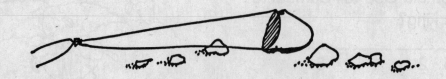

# 23. Jonathan's Secret Code

## 1 Samuel 19 & 20

Jonathan and David were good friends. Jonathan's father, King Saul, wanted to kill David, so David had to run away and hide. Jonathan used a secret code to tell David whether it was safe for him to come back to the king's house.

While David hid in the field, Jonathan would shoot three arrows. If Jonathan told his armor bearer that the arrows were closer than the spot where David was hiding it meant:

(Use the Morse code to find the meaning.)

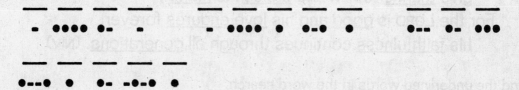

If he said that the arrows were farther than where David was it meant:

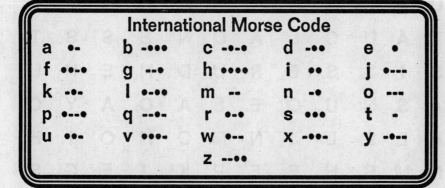

### International Morse Code

| | | | | | | | | | |
|---|---|---|---|---|---|---|---|---|---|
| a | •- | b | -••• | c | -•-• | d | -•• | e | • |
| f | ••-• | g | --• | h | •••• | i | •• | j | •--- |
| k | -•- | l | •-•• | m | -- | n | -• | o | --- |
| p | •--• | q | --•- | r | •-• | s | ••• | t | - |
| u | ••- | v | •••- | w | •-- | x | -••- | y | -•-- |
| | | | | z | --•• | | | | |

# 24. Psalm 100

Shout for joy to the LORD, all the earth.
   Worship the LORD with gladness;
   come before him with joyful songs.
Know that the LORD is God.
   It is he who made us, and we are his;
   we are his people, the sheep of his pasture.
Enter his gates with thanksgiving
   and his courts with praise;
   give thanks to him and praise his name.
For the LORD is good and his love endures forever;
   his faithfulness continues through all generations. (NIV)

Find the underlined words in the word search.

```
I  L  F  O  E  L  P  O  E  P  V  E
T  H  A  N  K  S  G  I  V  I  N  G
T  O  I  S  B  N  E  W  O  N  K  M
E  N  T  E  R  O  J  O  L  G  Y  A
R  P  H  T  P  I  H  S  R  O  W  D
U  R  F  A  H  T  R  A  E  D  F  E
T  A  U  G  L  A  D  N  E  S  S  T
S  I  L  S  E  R  U  D  N  E  H  U
A  S  N  U  Q  E  L  A  O  A  Y  O
P  E  E  L  J  N  M  O  N  O  I  H
N  M  S  H  E  E  P  K  J  E  G  S
H  I  S  O  N  G  S  T  R  U  O  C
```

# 25. Psalm 117

Psalm 117 is the shortest psalm. It is also the shortest chapter in the Bible. Can you memorize it?

O praise the LORD, all ye nations:
　　praise him, all ye people.
For his merciful kindness is great toward us:
　　and the truth of the LORD endureth forever.
Praise ye the LORD.

Write your own psalm. First write "Praise the Lord!" Then write two things that you thank or praise him for. Then write "Praise the Lord!"

_____

_____

_____

_____

_____

_____

_____

# 26. A Lame Boy at the King's Table

## 2 Samuel 9

When David became king he asked if there were any members of Saul's family still living. He was told that Mephibosheth, Jonathan's lame son, was still living. David sent for Mephibosheth, who came and bowed down before the king.

Follow the maze of letters to find out what David said to Mephibosheth.

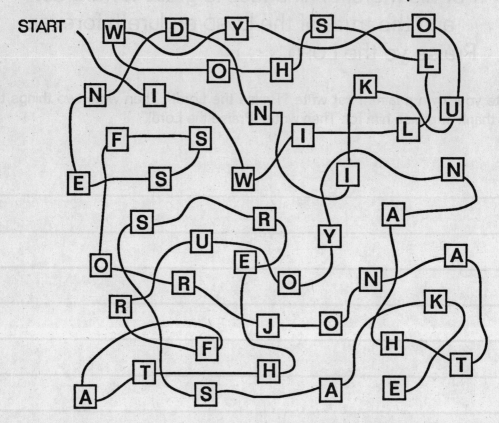

Add or subtract the number of letters written under each line.

| A B C D E F G H I J K L M N O P Q R S T U V W X Y Z |
|---|

David also told Mephibosheth, "You shall ___ ___ ___
                                          D+1 C-2 R+2

at my ___ ___ ___ ___ ___ like one of my ___ ___ ___ ___."
      W-3 B-1 A+1 J+2 H-3                 Q+2 P-1 M+1 V-3

34

# 27. King David's Sin

One evening King David was walking on the flat roof of the palace. He looked down and saw a beautiful woman in her garden. He found out that her name was Bathsheba and that she was married to a soldier named Uriah.

David wanted to marry Bathsheba, but he couldn't because she had a husband. So David sent a terrible message to Joab, the commander of his army.

Cross out these letters: C, G, J, K, M, Q, V, X, Y, Z. The remaining letters spell the message.

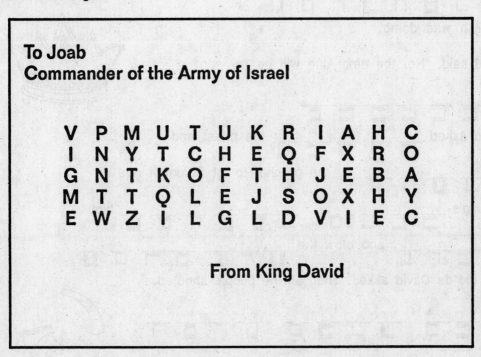

**To Joab**
**Commander of the Army of Israel**

```
V P M U T U K R I A H C
I N Y T C H E Q F X R O
G N T K O F T H J E B A
M T T Q L E J S O X H Y
E W Z I L G L D V I E C
```

**From King David**

David committed two sins: murder and adultery.

God sent the prophet Nathan to show David his sins. David was very sorry for his sins and asked God to forgive him. God forgave David, but one of his punishments was that David and Bathsheba's first son died.

You can read about David's repentance in Psalm 51.

# 28. Solomon on David's Throne

## 1 Kings 1

King David was very ⬚⬚⬚.

⬚⬚⬚⬚⬚⬚⬚⬚, his son, tried to make himself ⬚⬚⬚⬚.

⬚⬚⬚⬚⬚⬚⬚⬚⬚ told David what Adonijah was doing.

David said, "No, the next king will be my son ⬚⬚⬚⬚⬚⬚⬚."

David asked ⬚⬚⬚⬚⬚⬚ the priest and ⬚⬚⬚⬚⬚⬚⬚ the prophet to let Solomon ride on the king's ⬚⬚⬚⬚, ⬚⬚⬚⬚⬚⬚ him with ⬚⬚⬚, and blow the ⬚⬚⬚⬚⬚⬚⬚⬚.

They did as David asked. Then all the people shouted,

"⬚⬚⬚ ⬚⬚⬚⬚ ⬚⬚⬚⬚ ⬚⬚⬚⬚⬚⬚⬚!"

Adonijah was ⬚⬚⬚⬚⬚⬚⬚ when he heard what had happened. He grabbed the ⬚⬚⬚⬚⬚ of the ⬚⬚⬚⬚⬚ and begged Solomon for his life.

Solomon showed him ⬚⬚⬚⬚⬚⬚.

| A | B | C |
|---|---|---|
| D | E | F |
| G | H | I |

| J | K | L |
|---|---|---|
| M | N | O |
| P | Q | R |

| S | T | U |
|---|---|---|
| V | W | X |
| Y | Z | |

# 29. Elijah

Elijah, the prophet, performed many miracles. Some of those miracles are found in 1 Kings 17 and 18. The following words are taken from those chapters. Find the words in the word search.

```
W I D O W L Z W T U C A
B D L P A B A R R E L K
U O E E R T R X L T O O
L O M S E O E E A B U O
L W R R E R P R A Y D R
O B A D I A H H B D E B
C D C F X R A V E N S O
K I S H O N T W X T O I
X E L I J A H R A I N L
```

ELIJAH
PROPHET
AHAB
DEW
RAIN
BROOK
RAVENS
ZAREPHATH
WIDOW
BARREL
MEAL
OIL
BREAD
SON
DIE

BED
PRAY
OBADIAH
BAAL
CARMEL
WOOD
BULLOCK
CUT
ALTAR
FIRE
WATER
KISHON
SEA
CLOUD

# 30. An Enemy and a Friend

## 1 Kings 19

Queen _ _ _ _ _ _ _, King _ _ _ _'s wife, was angry that Elijah had shown that his God was more powerful than the prophets of Baal. Jezebel threatened to kill Elijah.

Elijah ran away to the desert. He was tired, _ _ _ _ _ _ _ and discouraged. God sent an angel to feed and comfort him.

Then the Lord gave him a new job. Elijah was to anoint new kings for Israel and Judah and a new prophet to take his own place. The _ _ _ _ also encouraged him by telling him that there were seven thousand men in Israel who had never bowed to the _ _ _ _ Baal.

Elijah was refreshed and encouraged and went to do the Lord's will.

Elijah found _ _ _ _ _ _ _ plowing a field. Elijah took his cloak and threw it around Elisha's shoulders. Elisha knew this meant he should leave his home and become a prophet like Elijah.

Elijah trained Elisha, and Elisha was an encouraging friend to Elijah.

Write the missing words in the boxes below.

# 31. Elijah's Departure

## 2 Kings 2

Elisha followed the prophet Elijah wherever he went. One day Elijah asked, "What can I do for you before I leave?" Solve the puzzle to find out what Elisha asked for.

Take the letters in each column and put them in the same order in the squares above the column. A black square marks the end of a word.

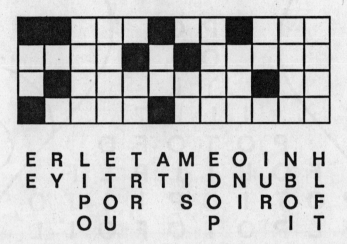

```
E  R  L  E  T  A  M  E  O  I  N  H
E  Y  I  T  R  T  I  D  N  U  B  L
   P  O  R     S  O  I  R  O  F
   O  U        P        I  T
```

Solve the second puzzle to find out how Elijah went to heaven.

```
H  O  A  S  C  H  A  R  I  O  T  I  A  N  D  C
A  M  R     E  S  D  O  F  O  F  K  R  E  I  M
   I  E     A  N  W  H  T  R  O  W  I  H  D
   N        A        I        L        N
```

Elisha watched Elijah go up to heaven. Then he picked up Elijah's cloak and took over Elijah's work as prophet to Israel.

# 32. The Pot of Oil

In 2 Kings 4 we read the story of a poor woman whom Elisha helped with a pot of oil.

How many times can you find "POT OF OIL" in the word search?

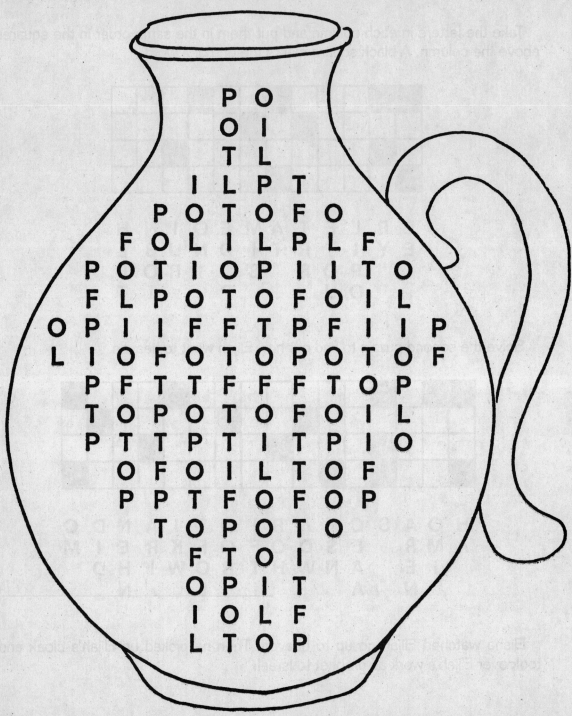

# 33. The Woman of Shunem

## 2 Kings 4

Unscramble the words below to find a list of things that the Shunammite woman gave to Elisha to make his stay more comfortable.

1. ERDAB
2. BREAHMC
3. EDB
4. TEALB
5. OLSOT
6. LEADNCTCSKI

To thank the Shunammite woman for her hospitality, Elisha gave her a promise.

Use the code to find the promise. The first number indicates the word in the list and the second number indicates which letter in that word (for example, 2-5 is the second word, the fifth letter "B").

Y __ u   W __ __ __   __ __ v __
5-3     6-9 4-4 6-5    2-2 1-4   3-2

__   __ __ __ .
4-2   5-1 5-4 6-3

# 34. A Slave Girl Helps Her Sick Master

## 2 Kings 5

Naaman was a brave and powerful captain in the Syrian army. The sad thing about Naaman was that he had a sickness called leprosy. His wife's Israelite slave girl felt sorry for her master and wished he could get better.

What did the little girl say Naaman should do to get better?

$\overline{2\text{-}4}$ $\overline{5\text{-}3}$ $\quad\overline{5\text{-}2}$ $\overline{5\text{-}3}$ $\quad\overline{5\text{-}2}$ $\overline{3\text{-}4}$ $\overline{5\text{-}5}$

$\overline{1\text{-}2}$ $\overline{3\text{-}2}$ $\overline{5\text{-}3}$ $\overline{1\text{-}2}$ $\quad\overline{3\text{-}4}$ $\overline{5\text{-}5}$ $\overline{5\text{-}2}$ $\quad\overline{4\text{-}4}$ $\overline{4\text{-}3}$

$\overline{4\text{-}4}$ $\overline{4\text{-}2}$ $\overline{3\text{-}2,}$ $\overline{1\text{-}5}$ $\overline{5\text{-}5}$ $\overline{2\text{-}3}$

What did the prophet tell Naaman to do?

$\overline{3\text{-}1}$ $\overline{1\text{-}5}$ $\overline{4\text{-}2}$ $\overline{3\text{-}4}$ $\quad\overline{4\text{-}4}$ $\overline{4\text{-}3}$ $\quad\overline{5\text{-}4}$ $\overline{5\text{-}3}$ $\overline{3\text{-}2}$ $\overline{4\text{-}5}$ $\overline{1\text{-}5}$ $\overline{4\text{-}3}$

$\overline{4\text{-}2}$ $\overline{5\text{-}5}$ $\overline{2\text{-}1}$ $\overline{5\text{-}5}$ $\overline{4\text{-}3}$ $\quad\overline{5\text{-}2}$ $\overline{4\text{-}4}$ $\overline{3\text{-}3}$ $\overline{5\text{-}5}$ $\overline{4\text{-}2}$

What happened when Naaman obeyed the prophet?

$\overline{3\text{-}4}$ $\overline{5\text{-}5}$ $\quad\overline{3\text{-}1}$ $\overline{1\text{-}5}$ $\quad\overline{4\text{-}2}$ $\quad\overline{3\text{-}4}$ $\overline{5\text{-}5}$ $\overline{1\text{-}5}$ $\overline{2\text{-}3}$ $\overline{5\text{-}5}$ $\overline{4\text{-}5}$

| | | | | | |
|---|---|---|---|---|---|
| **5** | A | B | C | D | E |
| **4** | F | G | H | I | J |
| **3** | K | L | M | N | O |
| **2** | P | Q | R | S | T |
| **1** | U | V | W | X | Y |
| | **1** | **2** | **3** | **4** | **5** |

To find the correct letter in the graph go across the bottom line till you get to the first number in the code (5-4). The second number indicates the number of rows you need to go up (5-4). 5-4 is the letter "J."

# 35. The Young King
## 2 Chronicles 22–24

Joash was very young when he became king of Judah. Use the code below to answer the questions.

**Where did Joash live during the first six years of his life?**

 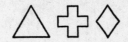 

__ __    __ __ __    __ __ __ __ __ __

**How old was Joash when he became king?**

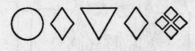

__ __ __ __ __

**What did Joash command to be done?**

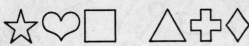 

__ __ __    __ __ __    __ __ __ __ __ __

| ◇ | ☆ | ✚ | ♡ | ⬭D | ✧ | ❄ | ○ | △ | ▽ | □ |
|---|---|---|---|----|----|----|---|---|---|---|
| E | F | H | I | L  | M  | N  | P | S | T | V | X |

43

# 36. The Lost Book

## 2 Chronicles 34

What happened when King Josiah ordered the temple to be cleaned?

Follow the maze of letters.

1. __ __ __ __ __

   __ __ __ __ __

   __ __ __

   __ __ __ __

   __ __

   __ __ __

   __ __ __ __ .

2. __ __ __ __ __

   __ __ __ __

   __ __ __

   __ __ __ __

   __ __

   __ __ __

   __ __ __ __ __ __ .

# 37. The Babylonian Captivity

Add or subtract the number of letters written under each line.

The people of Judah turned away from God and again began to

serve $\underset{\text{K-2}}{\text{I}}\ \underset{\text{E-1}}{\text{D}}\ \underset{\text{L+3}}{\text{O}}\ \underset{\text{M-1}}{\text{L}}\ \underset{\text{Q+2}}{\text{S}}$.

The prophet $\underset{\text{I+1}}{\text{J}}\ \underset{\text{H-3}}{\text{E}}\ \underset{\text{O+3}}{\text{R}}\ \underset{\text{D+1}}{\text{E}}\ \underset{\text{O-2}}{\text{M}}\ \underset{\text{L-3}}{\text{I}}\ \underset{\text{C-2}}{\text{A}}\ \underset{\text{F+2}}{\text{H}}$ warned the people

that their evil ways would bring trouble. They didn't listen.

King $\underset{\text{O-1}}{\text{N}}\ \underset{\text{D+1}}{\text{E}}\ \underset{\text{D-2}}{\text{B}}\ \underset{\text{S+2}}{\text{U}}\ \underset{\text{F-3}}{\text{C}}\ \underset{\text{E+3}}{\text{H}}\ \underset{\text{E-4}}{\text{A}}\ \underset{\text{H-4}}{\text{D}}\ \underset{\text{K+3}}{\text{N}}\ \underset{\text{H-3}}{\text{E}}\ \underset{\text{X+2}}{\text{Z}}\ \underset{\text{Y+1}}{\text{Z}}\ \underset{\text{C-2}}{\text{A}}\ \underset{\text{S-1}}{\text{R}}$

fought the people of Judah and won. He took the valuables out of

the $\underset{\text{W-3}}{\text{T}}\ \underset{\text{G-2}}{\text{E}}\ \underset{\text{N-1}}{\text{M}}\ \underset{\text{O+1}}{\text{P}}\ \underset{\text{J+2}}{\text{L}}\ \underset{\text{B+3}}{\text{E}}$ and burned it.

The people were taken as captives to

$\underset{\text{D-2}}{\text{B}}\ \underset{\text{B-1}}{\text{A}}\ \underset{\text{A+1}}{\text{B}}\ \underset{\text{Z-1}}{\text{Y}}\ \underset{\text{J+2}}{\text{L}}\ \underset{\text{R-3}}{\text{O}}\ \underset{\text{J+4}}{\text{N}}$.

Jeremiah prophesied that the people would return to Jerusalem

after $\underset{\text{Q+2}}{\text{S}}\ \underset{\text{F-1}}{\text{E}}\ \underset{\text{U+1}}{\text{V}}\ \underset{\text{C+2}}{\text{E}}\ \underset{\text{P-2}}{\text{N}}\ \underset{\text{P+4}}{\text{T}}\ \underset{\text{X+1}}{\text{Y}}$ years.

# 38. Homesick Jews

The people of Judah, now called Jews, were captives in Babylon. There were Babylonian idols all around them, but the Jews only wanted to serve God. God sent prophets to encourage the people.

The people taught their children about God and Jerusalem. They often sang songs about Jerusalem, which is also called Zion. One of the songs is found in Psalm 137.

By the <u>rivers</u> of Babylon we sat and <u>wept</u>
   when we remembered Zion.
There on the <u>poplars</u>
   we hung our <u>harps</u>,
for there our <u>captors</u> asked us for songs,
   our tormentors demanded <u>songs</u> of joy;
   , they said, "Sing us one of the songs of <u>Zion</u>!"
How can we sing the songs of the <u>LORD</u>
   while in a foreign <u>land</u>?
If I forget you, O Jerusalem,
   may my right <u>hand</u> forget its skill.
May my tongue cling to the roof of my <u>mouth</u>
   if I do not remember you,
if I do not consider Jerusalem
   my highest <u>joy</u>. (NIV)

Fit the underlined words into the stack-a-word puzzle below.

# 39. The Hand That Wrote on the Wall
## Daniel 5

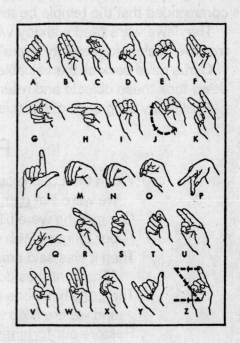

The American Manual Alphabet uses different finger positions to spell out words. Practice spelling the alphabet with your hand.

Use the manual alphabet to solve the puzzle.

Daniel was called in to the king's banquet to interpret the writing on the wall. Daniel told the king about his sin and punishment.

What was King Belshazzar's sin?

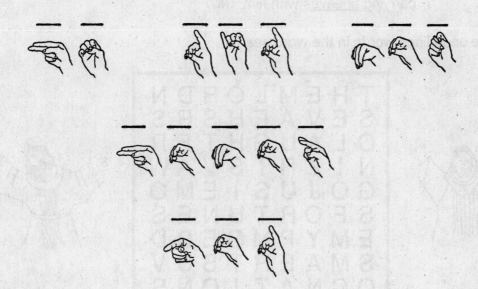

# 40. Return to Zion

King Cyrus was a friend to the captive Jews. Cyrus gave honor to God and commanded that the temple be rebuilt in Jerusalem.

The Jews were filled with joy when they heard this news. They had been away from Jerusalem for seventy years and were glad to go back.

Cyrus gave back all the valuables that had been removed from the temple. The Jews took these objects and returned to Jerusalem, which is also called Zion.

Again they sang a song, but this time it was a song of joy.

## Psalm 126

When the LORD brought back the <u>captives</u> to Zion,
    we were like <u>men</u> who <u>dreamed</u>.
Our <u>mouths</u> were filled with <u>laughter</u>,
    our tongues with songs of joy.
Then it was said among the <u>nations</u>,
    "The LORD has done great things for <u>them</u>."
The <u>LORD</u> has done great things for <u>us</u>,
    and we are filled with <u>joy</u>.
Restore our <u>fortunes</u>, O LORD,
    like <u>streams</u> in the Negev.
Those who sow in <u>tears</u>
    will reap with <u>songs</u> of joy.
He who goes out weeping,
    carrying <u>seed</u> to <u>sow</u>,
will return with songs of joy,
    carrying <u>sheaves</u> with him. (NIV)

Find the underlined words in the word search.

```
T H E M L O R D N
S E V A E H S R S
O L A U G H T E R
N I Z R T S V A W
G O J U S I E M O
S F O R T U N E S
E M Y P M G E D D
S M A E R T S U V
O C N A T I O N S
```

# 41. Prophets Predict Baby's Birth

Prophets are men whom God sent to tell the people special messages. Many prophets told the people about a baby's birth. Dial-a-Message to find out what they said about the baby.

3-3  6-3  7-2     8-2  6-2  8-1  6-3     8-2  7-3     2-1

2-3  4-2  4-3  5-3  3-1  ·  4-3  7-3     2-2  6-3  7-2  6-2

Isaiah 9:6

2-3  2-1  5-3  5-3     4-2  4-3  7-3     6-2  2-1  6-1  3-2

4-3  6-1  6-1  2-1  6-2  8-2  3-2  5-3

Isaiah 7:14

2-2  3-2  4-2  6-3  5-3  3-1     8-1  4-2  9-3

5-2  4-3  6-2  4-1     2-3  6-3  6-1  3-2  8-1  4-2

Zechariah 9:9

2-2  3-2  8-1  4-2  5-3  3-2  4-2  3-2  6-1  . . .  6-3  8-2  8-1

6-3  3-3     8-1  4-2  3-2  3-2     7-3  4-2  2-1  5-3  5-3

4-2  3-2     2-3  6-3  6-1  3-2

Micah 5:2

**How to Dial-a-Message:**
The first number tells you what circle to look at on the dial. The second number tells you which letter to write down (for example, 7-2 is "R," the second letter on the 7 circle).

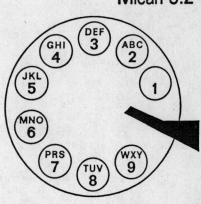

# New Testament

# 42. Joseph's Dream

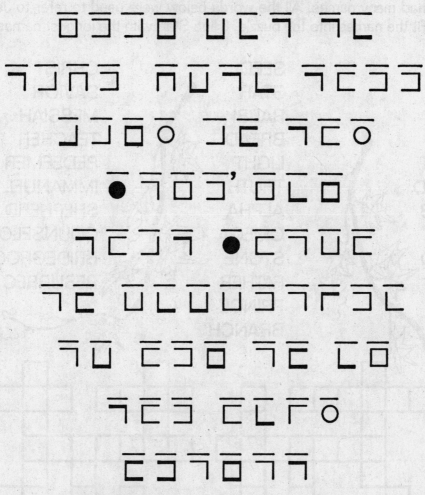

| A | C | D | | M | N | O | | | |
|---|---|---|---|---|---|---|---|---|---|
| E | F | H | | P | R | S | | ● | ○ |
| I | K | L | | T | U | V | | **W** | **Y** |

# 43. And His Name Shall Be Called . . .

Jesus had many names. All the words below were used to refer to Jesus in the Bible. Fit the names into the puzzle. (Hint: Start with the longest names.)

GOD
SUN
WAY
ONE
ROOT
WORD
LAMB
GATE
LORD
KING
VINE
LIFE

SEED
STAR
RABBI
BREAD
LIGHT
TRUTH
ALPHA
OMEGA
STONE
FATHER
PRINCE
BRANCH

CHRIST
SAVIOR
MESSIAH
TEACHER
REDEEMER
IMMANUEL
SHEPHERD
COUNSELOR
BRIDEGROOM
RESURRECTION

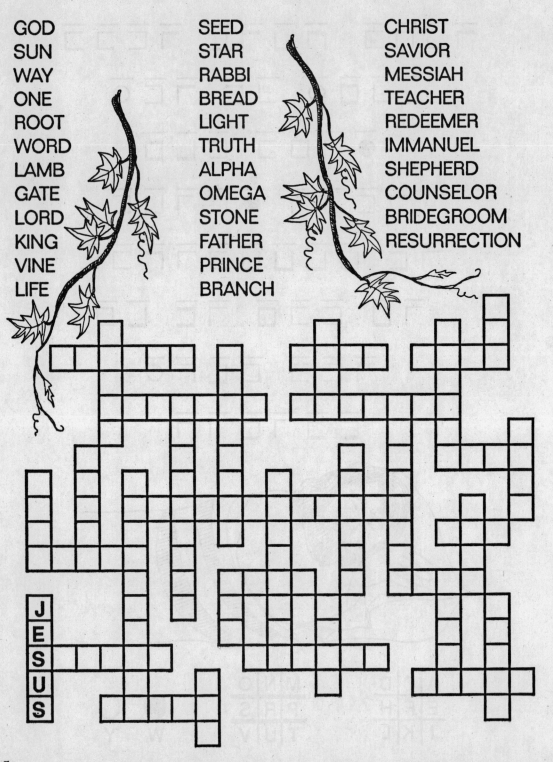

# 44. Wise Men Worship Jesus

Complete the addition problems inside the gifts. The missing numbers correspond to a letter. Use those letters to complete the sentences below.

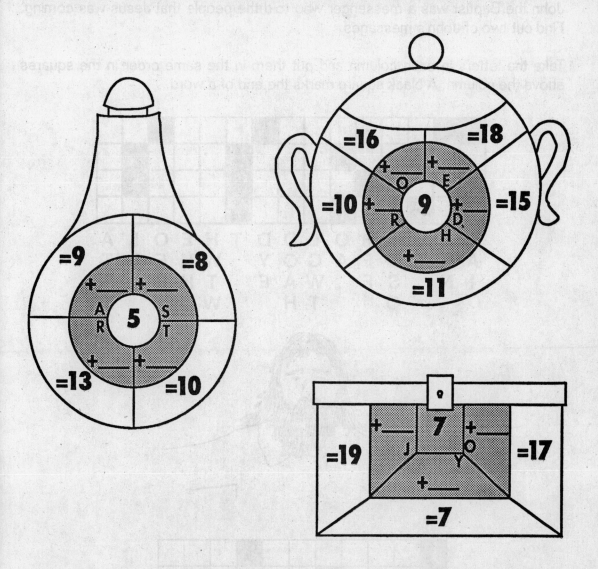

The wise men started their search for Jesus because of a _____.

3, 5, 4, 8

The wise men asked _____ for information about the new king.

2, 9, 1, 7, 6

Finding Jesus and worshiping him brought the wise men great_____.

12, 10, 0

# 45. John the Baptist

## God's Special Messenger

John the Baptist was a messenger who told the people that Jesus was coming. Find out two of John's messages.

Take the letters in each column and put them in the same order in the squares above the column. A black square marks the end of a word.

```
M B B E H O L D D D   T H E O L A
A K E O F A G O Y     W H E L T
  I N   S F   A G E   T H R   S
        O   W A   H   W O     D
              T
```

```
M R E P E N T N F O R
T H E A K I A G D O N
I   O F   H E H V E N
S         T   A N D
```

# 46. Fishers of Men
## Jesus' Disciples

Draw a line from the disciple's name to the statement about him.

Peter — a tax collector

Andrew — son of Zebedee and brother of James

James — also called Didymus

John — brother of John

Philip — his name means "rock"

Matthew — betrayed Jesus

Thomas — son of Alphaeus (also called "the Less")

James — Peter's brother

Simon — he brought Nathanael to Jesus

Judas — a Canaanite, also called Zelotes

Here are some Bible passages to help you.
Matthew 4:18–21; 10:2–4 (NIV); 16:17–18
Mark 3:14–19
John 1:43–51; 11:16
Acts 1:13

Which two names are missing from the list? _____ _____

# 47. The Beatitudes

Have you memorized the Beatitudes? They are found in Matthew 5:3–11.
Try doing the puzzle without looking up the passage in your Bible.

Blessed are the poor in (5): for theirs is the kingdom of heaven.
Blessed are they that (1 down): for they shall be comforted. Blessed
are the meek: for they shall inherit the (10). Blessed are they which
do (11) and thirst after righteousness: for they shall be filled. Blessed
are the merciful: for they shall obtain (1 across). Blessed are the (8)
in heart: for they shall see God. Blessed are the (7): for they shall be
called the (2) of God. Blessed are they which are persecuted for
righteousness' sake: for theirs is the kingdom of (3). Blessed are ye,
when men shall (6) you, and persecute you, and shall say all manner
of (9) against you falsely, for my (4).

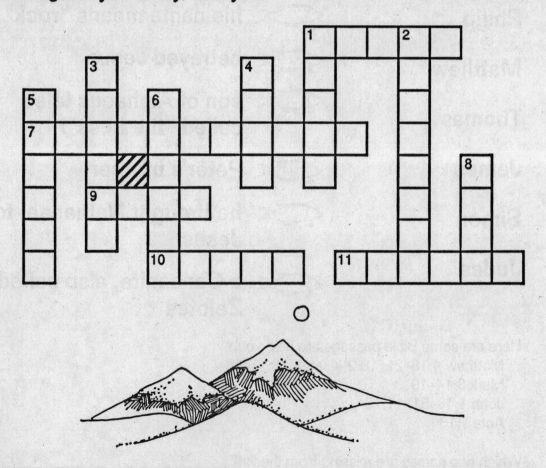

# 48. Sermon on the Mount

To find one of Jesus' messages from the Sermon on the Mount, write the first letter of each picture below it.

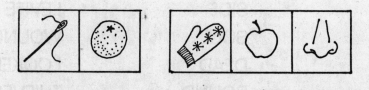

_ _     _ _ _

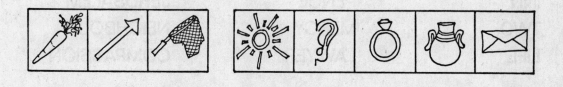

_ _ _     _ _ _ _ _

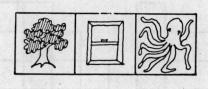

_ _ _

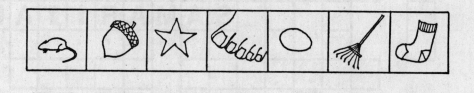

_ _ _ _ _ _ _

Matthew 6:24

# 49. The Good Samaritan

Read the story of the Good Samaritan in Luke 10:25–37. The following words are taken from that passage. Fit the words into the crossword puzzle.

| | | |
|---|---|---|
| DO | LOVE | PRIEST |
| GO | SIDE | LEVITE |
| ALL | SOUL | WOUNDS |
| LAW | DEAD | LOOKED |
| GOD | BOUND | THIEVES |
| OIL | BEAST | RAIMENT |
| INN | PENCE | JERUSALEM |
| TWO | MERCY | NEIGHBOUR |
| LIFE | LAWYER | COMPASSION |

# 50. The Foolish Rich Man

Jesus told a parable about a rich man who had more crops than he had storage room. He wanted to keep everything for himself, so he decided to build bigger barns. That way he wouldn't have to work as hard the next year. All he could think about was keeping everything (his treasures) for himself.

Starting at the arrow, cross out every other letter in the barn. Write the remaining letters down to find out what Jesus taught about treasures (Matt. 6:19–21).

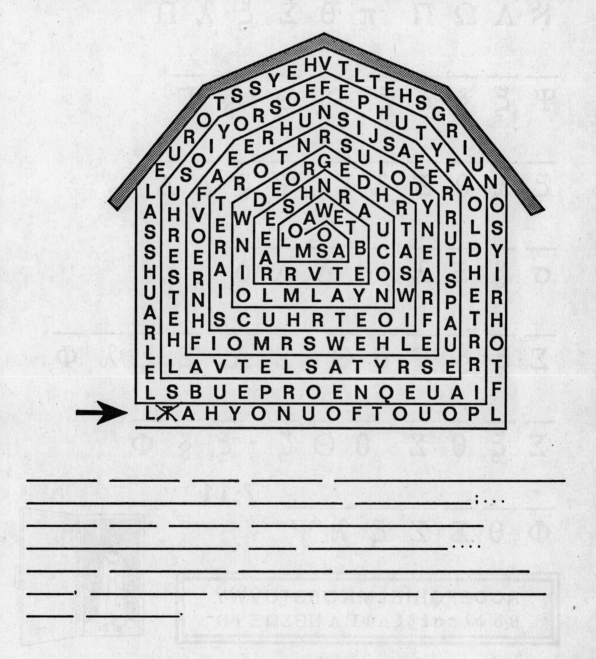

\_\_\_\_ \_\_\_ _____ _____

_____ _____ _____ ; . . .

_____ _____ _____

_____ _____ . . . .

_____ _____ _____

\_\_\_\_\_ ' _____ _____

\_\_\_\_ \_\_\_\_\_ .

# 51. Midnight Visitor

Did anyone ever knock on your door at midnight and ask for bread? That's what happened to a man in a story Jesus told. Read the story in Luke 11:5–10.

Use the code to find out what Jesus was teaching his disciples.

Ϗ Λ Ω Π π θ Σ ξ λ Π
*(Y O U R F A T H E R)*

Ψ ξ § δ ξ § Θ § Γ
*(W H I C H I S I N)*

ξ λ θ Ξ λ Γ Ψ § Δ Δ
*(H E A V E N W I L L)*

σ § Ξ λ σ Λ Λ φ
*(G I V E G O O D)*

Σ ξ § Γ σ Θ Σ Λ Σ ξ λ Φ
*(T H I N G S T O T H E M)*

Σ ξ θ Σ θ Θ ζ ξ § Φ .
*(T H A T A S K H I M)*

**7:11**

Φ θ Σ Σ ξ λ Ψ
*(M A T T H E W)*

| A | C | D | E | F | G | H | I | K | L | M | N | O | R | S | T | U | V | W | Y |
|---|---|---|---|---|---|---|---|---|---|---|---|---|---|---|---|---|---|---|---|
| θ | δ | φ | λ | π | σ | ξ | § | ζ | Δ | Φ | Γ | Λ | Π | Θ | Σ | Ω | Ξ | Ψ | Ϗ |

# 52. Jesus Calms the Storm

Find as many words as you can in the letters below. Go from left to right.

(STORM)SEASTILLOBEYWINDISHIPAWAKEPEACE

1. _____STORM_____

2. _____

3. _____

4. _____

5. _____

6. _____

7. _____

8. _____

9. _____

10. _____

11. _____

12. _____

13. _____

14. _____

15. _____

16. _____

17. _____

18. _____

19. _____

20. _____

**Super Word Finder!**

21. _____

22. _____

23. _____

24. _____

25. _____

# 53. Jesus Heals a Paralyzed Man

Four men brought their paralyzed friend to Jesus to be healed. They couldn't get near Jesus because there were so many people at the house where he was preaching. They took the paralyzed man up to the roof, made an opening in it, and lowered him down to Jesus. Jesus forgave the man's sins and healed him.

Circle the things that are different in the second picture.

# 54. Jairus's Daughter

What did Jesus tell Jairus to do when his daughter died?

To find out, write down every other letter from the circle below, beginning at the arrow ↓ and going clockwise.

_____  _____

_____  _____

____  ____  ____

____  ____

____  ____

Luke 8:50

# 55. Jesus Chooses Twelve Disciples

## Luke 6:12–16    Mark 6:7–13

Crowds followed Jesus from town to town as he taught and healed the people. One day Jesus chose twelve of these followers to be his special helpers.

Find the answers to questions 1 and 2 in the puzzle below. To find the answer to question 1, begin at the top arrow and write down each letter you come to. Then begin at the bottom arrow to find the answer to question 2.

1. What did Jesus do before he chose the 12?

_____

*To think about:*
What should you do before you make an important decision?

2. What did Jesus tell the disciples to do?

_____

*To think about:*
What special work has Jesus called you to do?

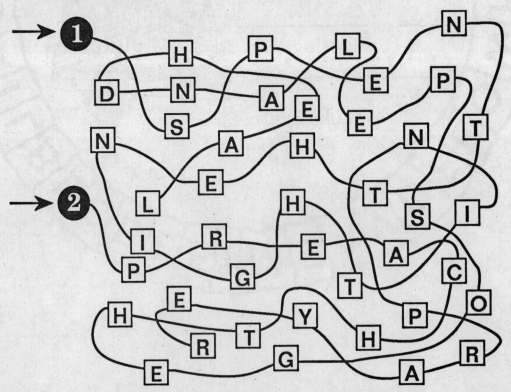

# 56. John's Question Answered
## Matthew 11

John the Baptist was in prison. He could not talk to Jesus or see what Jesus was doing. John sent some of his followers to Jesus to ask if Jesus was the promised Messiah.

Jesus told them to tell John what they saw.

```
T B H E E C B A L U I S N E D T S H E O E
U T H H A E S L T A S M E E E W N A M L E
K T T H H O E U L H E A P S E T R B S E A
L R I E E C V L E E D A B N L S E E S D S
T E H D E A D R E E A T F H H E E Y A T R
H T A H T E H D A E V A E D N A O R T E S
R E A E I N S A E N D D T Y O E T T H H E
A P V O E O B R E T L H I E E G V O E S D
P J E O L H I N S T P W R E E N A T C Y H
2 E 9 D
```

Write down every other letter starting with the "T."

_____ _____ _____ , _____ _____ _____ ,

_____ _____ _____ _____ , _____

_____ _____ , _____ _____ _____ ,

_____ _____ _____ _____ _____ _____ .


Write the remaining letters starting with the "B."

_____ _____ _____ _____ ____ , _____

_____ _____ : _____ _____ _____

_____ _____ _____ , _____ _____

_____ _____ _____ . _____

# 57. Jesus Heals on the Sabbath

## Matthew 12

Fill in the blanks using the opposite of the underlined word.

Jesus went to the synagogue on the Sabbath Day. A (<u>woman</u>) _____ with a withered hand was there. Jesus' (<u>friends</u>) _____ asked him, "Is it (<u>wrong</u>) _____ to (<u>injure</u>) _____ on the Sabbath?"

Jesus answered, "If your sheep falls into a pit on the Sabbath, won't you lift it (<u>in</u>) _____?"

Jesus said to the man, "Stretch out your hand." He stretched it out and it was like (<u>old</u>) _____.

Jesus' enemies went (<u>toward</u>) _____ plotting how they could kill Jesus.

Use the first letter of each picture to finish the message.

| 1 | 2 | | 3 | 4 | 5 | 6 | | 7 | 8 |
|---|---|---|---|---|---|---|---|---|---|

| 9 | 10 | 11 | | 12 | 13 | 14 | 15 | 16 | 17 | 18 |
|---|----|----|---|----|----|----|----|----|----|----|

11

9, 17

13, 16

3

14, 15

2, 4, 5, 7

10, 18

8

1, 6

12

# 58. The Sower

## Matthew 13:1–23

In the parable of the sower different things happen to the seed that was planted.
Look up the verses and explain the meaning of the four seeds.

seed by wayside—eaten by birds

verse 19 (meaning in your own words)_____

_____

seed on stony ground—scorched by sun

verse 21_____

_____

seed among thorns—choked by thorns

verse 22 _____

_____

seed in good ground—fruitful

verse 23 _____

_____

# 59. The Fishnet

"The kingdom of heaven is like a net that was let down into the lake and caught all kinds of fish" (Matt. 13:47 NIV).

Up, down, across, or diagonally—how many times can you find the word "FISH"?

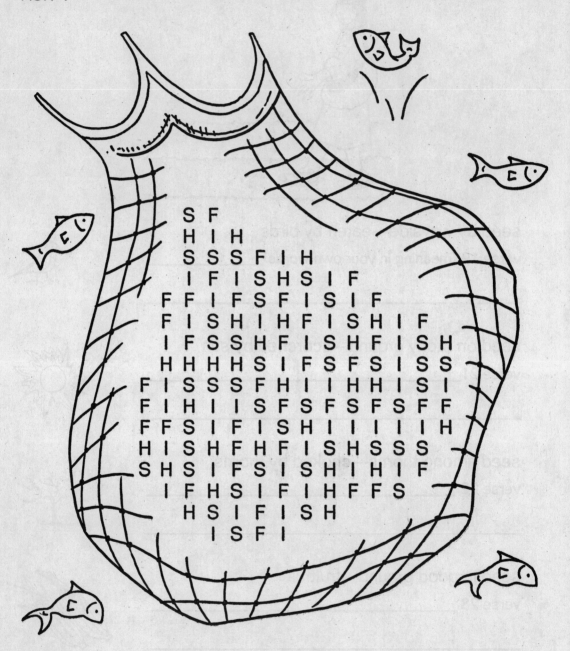

S F
H I H
S S S F I H
I F I S H S I F
F F I F S F I S I F
F I S H I H F I S H I F
I F S S H F I S H F I S H
H H H H S I F S F S I S S
F I S S S F H I I H H I S I
F I H I I S F S F S F S F F
F F S I F I S H I I I I I H
H I S H F H F I S H S S S
S H S I F S I S H I H I F
I F H S I F I H F F S
H S I F I S H
I S F I

# 60. Peter Walks on the Water

## Matthew 14:22–33

Read the Scripture passage.

Peter trusted Jesus and the Lord took care of him.

Use the code to find out what we should do.

$\overline{20}\ \overline{18}\ \overline{21}\ \overline{19}\ \overline{20}\quad \overline{9}\ \overline{14}\quad \overline{20}\ \overline{8}\ \overline{5}\quad \overline{12}\ \overline{15}\ \overline{18}\ \overline{4}$

$\overline{23}\ \overline{9}\ \overline{20}\ \overline{8}\quad \overline{1}\ \overline{12}\ \overline{12}\quad \overline{20}\ \overline{8}\ \overline{9}\ \overline{14}\ \overline{5}$

$\overline{8}\ \overline{5}\ \overline{1}\ \overline{18}\ \overline{20}\quad \overline{1}\ \overline{14}\ \overline{4}\quad \overline{12}\ \overline{5}\ \overline{1}\ \overline{14}$

$\overline{14}\ \overline{15}\ \overline{20}\quad \overline{21}\ \overline{14}\ \overline{20}\ \overline{15}\quad \overline{20}\ \overline{8}\ \overline{9}\ \overline{14}\ \overline{5}$

$\overline{15}\ \overline{23}\ \overline{14}\quad \overline{21}\ \overline{14}\ \overline{4}\ \overline{5}\ \overline{18}\ \overline{19}\ \overline{20}\ \overline{1}\ \overline{14}\ \overline{4}\ \overline{9}\ \overline{14}\ \overline{7}$

**3:5**

$\overline{16}\ \overline{18}\ \overline{15}\ \overline{22}\ \overline{5}\ \overline{18}\ \overline{2}\ \overline{19}$

| A | B | C | D | E | F | G | H | I | J | K | L | M |
|---|---|---|---|---|---|---|---|---|---|---|---|---|
| 1 | 2 | 3 | 4 | 5 | 6 | 7 | 8 | 9 | 10 | 11 | 12 | 13 |

| N | O | P | Q | R | S | T | U | V | W | X | Y | Z |
|---|---|---|---|---|---|---|---|---|---|---|---|---|
| 14 | 15 | 16 | 17 | 18 | 19 | 20 | 21 | 22 | 23 | 24 | 25 | 26 |

# 61. Jesus Feeds the Five Thousand

## Matthew 14:13–21

Jesus fed over five thousand people with five loaves of bread and two fish. Some words from this story are hidden in the basket. Try to find all the words listed below.

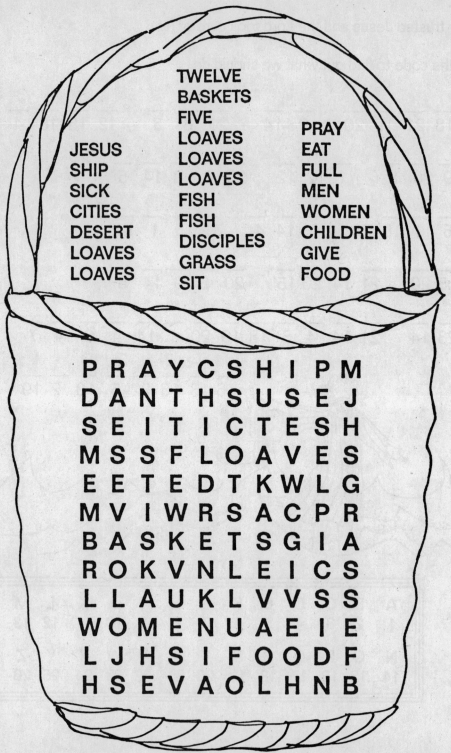

TWELVE
BASKETS
FIVE
LOAVES
LOAVES
LOAVES
FISH
FISH
DISCIPLES
GRASS
SIT

JESUS
SHIP
SICK
CITIES
DESERT
LOAVES
LOAVES

PRAY
EAT
FULL
MEN
WOMEN
CHILDREN
GIVE
FOOD

```
P R A Y C S H I P M
D A N T H S U S E J
S E I T I C T E S H
M S S F L O A V E S
E E T E D T K W L G
M V I W R S A C P R
B A S K E T S G I A
R O K V N L E I C S
L L A U K L V V S S
W O M E N U A E I E
L J H S I F O O D F
H S E V A O L H N B
```

# 62. Peter's Confession

## Matthew 16:13–20

Use the International Morse Code to decipher Peter's confession about Jesus.

### International Morse Code

| | | | | |
|---|---|---|---|---|
| a •– | b –••• | c –•–• | d –•• | e • |
| f ••–• | g ––• | h •••• | i •• | j •––– |
| k –•– | l •–•• | m –– | n –• | o ––– |
| p •––• | q ––•– | r •–• | s ••• | t – |
| u ••– | v •••– | w •–– | x –••– | y –•–– |
| | | z ––•• | | |

― ― ― ―   ― ― ―   ― ―   ― ― ― ―
 –  ••••  –––  ••–      •–  •–•  –      –  ••••  •

― ― ― ―   ― ― ―   ― ―   ― ― ―
–•–•  ••••  •–•  ••  •••  –      –  ••••  •      •••  –––  –•

― ― ―   ― ― ―   ― ―
–––  ••–•      –  ••••  •      •–••  ••  •••–  ••  –•  ––•

― ― ―
––•  –––  –••

# 63. Jesus' Transfiguration

## Matthew 17

Jesus was on a mountain with three of his disciples—Peter, James, and John. Suddenly Jesus' face shone as bright as the sun, and his clothes were as white as light. Moses and Elijah appeared and talked to Jesus. A bright cloud came over them, and God spoke.

Cross out the letters of the alphabet in order. The remaining letters will spell out what God said.

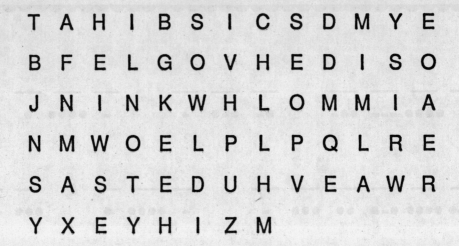

```
T A H I B S I C S D M Y E

B F E L G O V H E D I S O

J N I N K W H L O M M I A

N M W O E L P L P Q L R E

S A S T E D U H V E A W R

Y X E Y H I Z M
```

\_\_\_\_ \_\_\_ \_\_\_ \_\_\_

\_\_\_ \_\_\_\_\_ \_\_\_ \_\_\_\_ \_\_\_

\_\_\_\_ \_\_\_\_\_ . \_\_\_\_

\_\_\_\_ \_\_\_\_ .

# 64. Seventy Times Seven

Peter asked Jesus if he should forgive someone seven times. Jesus answered, "Not seven times but seventy times seven."

We should go on forgiving if a person is sorry for what he or she has done.

Use the code to find a verse about forgiveness. (See Col. 3:13.)

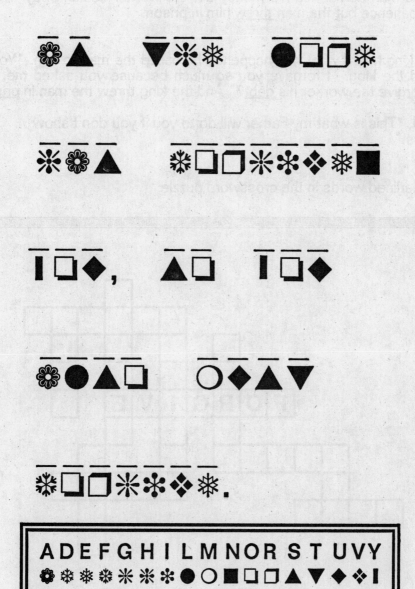

# 65. The Unforgiving Servant
## Matthew 18

Jesus told this parable or story to teach about forgiveness:

A man <u>owed</u> the king a lot of money. The man could not pay it back. He fell down before the king and asked him to be <u>patient</u>. The king felt <u>sorry</u> for him and let him go without having to pay the money.

Then the <u>man</u> went out and found another worker who owed the man a little bit of <u>money</u>. The man demanded his money but the worker couldn't pay. The worker asked for patience but the man <u>threw</u> him in prison.

When the <u>king</u> heard what had happened he called the man to him. "You <u>wicked</u> man," said the king. "I forgave you so much because you asked me. Couldn't you also forgive the worker his <u>debt</u>?" And the king threw the man in <u>prison</u>.

Jesus said, "This is what my Father will do to you if you don't show forgiveness."

Fit the underlined words in the crossword puzzle.

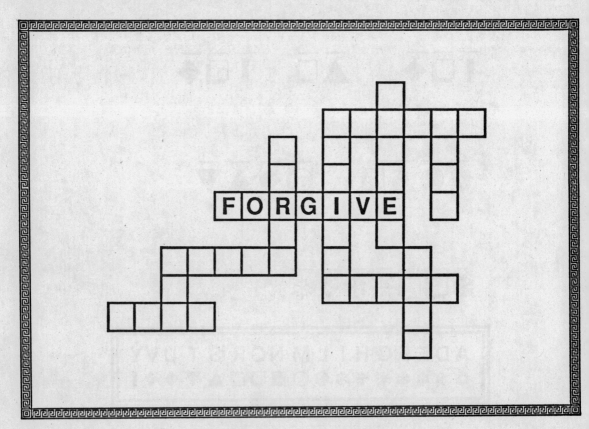

# 66. Jesus Welcomes the Children

Jesus said, "Let the little children come to me."

How many things can you find that start with the letter "B"?

# 67. Jesus Heals the Blind Man

Find as many words as you can in the letters below. Go from left to right. The first one is done for you.

**(BLIND)OPEACESONSATBEGODPRAISEEMAN**

1. _____BLIND_____

2. _____

3. _____

4. _____

5. _____

6. _____

7. _____

8. _____

9. _____

10. _____

11. _____

12. _____

13. _____

14. _____

15. _____

16. _____

17. _____

18. _____

19. _____

20. _____

**Super Word Finder!**

21. _____

22. _____

23. _____

24. _____

25. _____

# 68. The Parable of the Two Sons
## Matthew 21:28–32

A man had two sons.
He told the first son to go to work.
    What did the son *say?*_____

    What did the son *do?*_____
The man told the second son to go to work.
    What did this son *say?*_____

    What did he *do?*       _____
Which son showed his love for his father by obeying him?

Dial-a-Message to find out what Jesus said.

__ __     __ __ __     __ __ __ __
4-3 3-3     9-3 6-3 8-2     5-3 6-3 8-3 3-2

__ __,     __ __ __     __ __ __ __
6-1 3-2     9-3 6-3 8-2     9-1 4-3 5-3 5-3

__ __ __ __
6-3 2-2 3-2 9-3

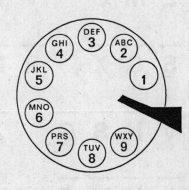

__ __.
6-1 3-2

How to Dial-a-Message:

The first number tells you what circle to look at on the dial. The second number tells you which letter to write down (for example, 6-1 is "M").

# 69. The Greatest Commandment

To find the greatest commandment write the next letter of the alphabet on the space. (Note: Use "A" after "Z.")

T H _ _ _ _     _ _ _ _ _
S G N T        R G Z K S

_ _ _ _     _ _ _ _     _ _ _ _
K N U D     S G D       K N Q C

_ _ _     _ _ _     _ _ _ _
S G X     F N C     V H S G

_ _ _     _ _ _     _ _ _ _ _ '
Z K K     S G X     G D Z Q S

_ _ _     _ _ _ _     _ _ _
Z M C     V H S G     Z K K

_ _ _     _ _ _ _ '     _ _ _
S G X     R N T K       Z M C

_ _ _ _     _ _ _     _ _ _
V H S G     Z K K     S G X

_ _ _ _ .
L H M C

What is the second greatest commandment? Matthew 22:39

_____

# 70. Jesus' Second Coming

In Matthew 24 Jesus told his disciples something about the time of his return. Solve the puzzle to find out what he said.

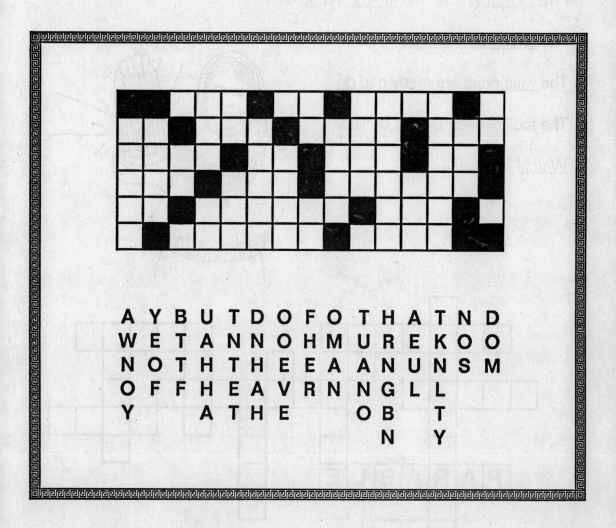

```
A Y B U T D O F O T H A T N D
W E T A N N O H M U R E K O O
N O T H T H E E A A N U N S M
O F F H E A V R N N G L L
Y     A T H E     O B   T
                  N     Y
```

Place each column of letters in the same order in the spaces above it. A black square marks the end of a word.

# 71. A Parable

Five wise virgins with lamps and oil

Five foolish virgins with lamps and no oil

The bridegroom comes!

The wise ones are ready and go

The foolish ones are left behind

Watch! Be ready!

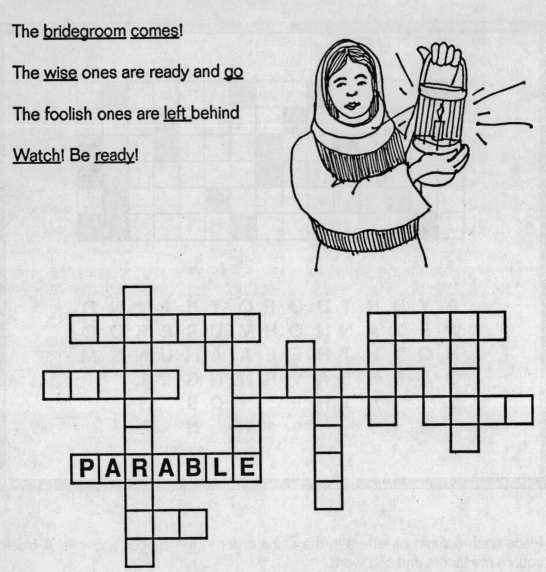

Fit the underlined words in the puzzle.

# 72. Mary Anoints Jesus' Feet

## John 12

When people walked along the roads in Bible times, dust would get inside their sandals and make their feet dirty. Therefore it was the custom to wash their feet when they entered someone's house.

Mary decided to wash Jesus' feet for him. But she did not use water. Mary poured some expensive perfume on Jesus' feet. Then she wiped his feet with her long hair. She did this to show her love for him.

What did Mary see when she looked at Jesus' feet? Did she see the dust? Did she see sores and calluses from walking many miles to tell people about God? Maybe Mary thought about the words of the prophet Isaiah.

Solve the puzzle to see what Isaiah 52:7 says.

Cross out these letters: C, J, K, Q, V, X, Y, Z.

CHOWQBEAUTIFULXUPONJ
THEZMOUNTAINSCAREYTHE
KFEETVOFXHIMJTHATK
QBRINGSYGOODJTIDINGSV

# 73. The Last Supper

Below are some sentences taken from Matthew 26:17–30. Fill in the blanks to find the answers for the crossword puzzle.

I will keep the (5)_____ at thy house with my disciples.

One of you shall (1)_____ me.

Take, eat; this is my (6)_____.

(4)_____ ye all of it.

For this is my (3)_____ of the new testament, which is

(2)_____ for many for the remission of sins.

# 74. Peter's Denial

Write down every other letter starting with the "L" to find two things Peter said on the night Jesus was arrested.

\_ \_ \_ \_ \_ ,   \_   \_ \_ \_ \_ \_ \_ \_

\_ \_ \_ \_   \_ \_ \_ '

\_ \_ \_   \_ \_ \_ \_   \_ \_

\_ \_ \_ \_ \_ \_   \_ \_ \_ \_   \_ \_

\_ \_ \_ \_ ,   \_   \_ \_   \_ \_ \_

\_ \_ \_ \_   \_ \_ \_ \_   \_ \_ \_ \_ .

START

# 75. Christ Died for Our Sins

For Christ died for sins
   once for all,
the righteous for the unrighteous,
   to bring you to God.
He was put to death in the body
   but made alive by the Spirit.

                    1 Peter 3:18 (NIV)

Find all the words of the verse in the
word search.

```
B C P E T E R O F H Y
R U D O H G I D E I D
F A T I N T G T C Y O
M O I I T C H H N O B
U N R I G H T E O U S
S B I F O R E V I L A
G T P I N I O P E L W
O A S N I S U F N A O
D E A T H T S N E H T
```

# 76. He Is Risen!

You killed the author of life, but

\_\_\_ _____ \_\_\_

\_\_\_\_\_ \_\_\_ \_\_\_\_\_.

\_\_\_\_ 3:15 (NIV)

Fill in the blanks using the alphabet code below.

7, 15, 4
18, 1, 9, 19, 5, 4
8, 9, 13
6, 18, 15, 13
20, 8, 5
4, 5, 1, 4
1, 3, 20, 19

| A | B | C | D | E | F | G | H | I | J | K | L | M |
|---|---|---|---|---|---|---|---|---|---|---|---|---|
| 1 | 2 | 3 | 4 | 5 | 6 | 7 | 8 | 9 | 10 | 11 | 12 | 13 |

| N | O | P | Q | R | S | T | U | V | W | X | Y | Z |
|---|---|---|---|---|---|---|---|---|---|---|---|---|
| 14 | 15 | 16 | 17 | 18 | 19 | 20 | 21 | 22 | 23 | 24 | 25 | 26 |

# 77. Pentecost

The words below are taken from Acts 2, where we read the story of Pentecost. Circle the words as you find them in the puzzle.

```
P P R O S E L Y T E S A S S W
T A T N E P E R C Y R E N E I
H M E S O P O T A M I A A U N
O P E T E R E Y P I I T I G D
U H S S D F B L P B G P H N E
S Y G A L I L E A N S Y T O Z
A L V O L R V R D M N G R T I
N I J U D E A J O E I E A H T
D A R P E N T E C O S T P X P
R P O N T U S W I T H R E E A
O R O M E D E S A I S A X S B
L E G A U G N A L S E T E R C
```

| | | |
|---|---|---|
| PENTECOST | LANGUAGE | LORD |
| GALILEANS | PARTHIANS | WIND |
| MEDES | ELAMITES | TONGUES |
| MESOPOTAMIA | JUDEA | FIRE |
| CAPPADOCIA | PONTUS | REPENT |
| ASIA | PHRYGIA | BAPTIZED |
| PAMPHYLIA | EGYPT | SINS |
| LIBYA | CYRENE | PETER |
| ROME | JEWS | THREE |
| PROSELYTES | CRETES | THOUSAND |
| ARABIANS | DAVID | |

# 78. Ananias and Sapphira

Read Acts 4:32–37; 5:1–11 (NIV).

Circle the correct answer in each sentence.

Ananias and Sapphira sold (their cow, some land, their house).

Ananias brought (some of the money, all of the money, none of the money) to the apostles for the church.

Ananias and Sapphira acted as if they were giving (some of the money, all of the money, none of the money).

(Barnabas, Peter, Paul) asked Ananias if he was lying.

Ananias was lying and he (went home, said he was sorry, died).

Sapphira came to Peter and she (knew, did not know) that her husband was dead.

Peter questioned her because he (wanted all the money, knew she did not agree with her husband, wanted to know if she was lying). Sapphira lied also.

Peter said, "Those who have buried your husband are at the door and they shall carry you out also." Sapphira fell down, struck dead by the power of (God, Peter, lightning).

Proverbs 19:22: Better to be poor than a liar.

Write out Proverbs 12:22. _____

_____

_____

# 79. Paul Shipwrecked

Paul was a prisoner on a ship bound for Rome. A storm wrecked the ship and everyone floated to an island. While everyone was drying off by a fire a poisonous snake bit Paul. To find out what happened to Paul read the story in Acts 27 and 28:1–16.

Unscramble the words taken from this story. Place the circled letters on the lines at the bottom to find out what Paul told the guards.

1. PHIS     _ _ _ ◯ _

2. ELBW     ◯ _ _ _

3. ESA      _ _ ◯ _

4. AYTIL    _ _ _ _ ◯

5. DWSIN    _ _ ◯ _ _

6. AMITEL   _ _ ◯ _ _ _

7. EVPRI    ◯ _ _ _ _

8. REIF     _ _ _ ◯

9. DRAGU    ◯ _ _ _ _

10. PREOS   _ ◯ _ _ _

11. LIDSSORE  _ _ _ _ ◯ _ _ _

_ _ _ _ _ _ _ _ _ _ _ _ _.

Acts 27:25

# 80. Letters from a Prisoner

## Acts 28

As a prisoner in Rome, Paul was allowed to live by himself with only a soldier to guard him.

Paul called together the leaders of the church in Rome and told them his story. He said it was because of the "hope of Israel" that he was bound in chains. Who was Paul talking about? _____

Paul remained in his own house for two years, preaching and writing letters of encouragement to other people and churches.

Unscramble the books of the Bible that Paul wrote as letters.

| | |
|---|---|
| **1 & 2** NISSANLASTOHE | SHEEPNAIS |
| **1 & 2** ACTSINHINOR | SNORMA |
| PIPILANSHPI | MELONHIP |
| **1 & 2** HIMOTYT | STUIT |
| SNICALSOOS | SLINGATAA |

Use the code to find out how Paul ended some of his letters.

The ＿＿＿＿＿ of our ＿＿＿＿
   H-1 P+2 D-3 G-4 A+4     O-3 M+2 S-1 C+1

＿＿＿＿＿ ＿＿＿＿＿＿ be
F+4 I-4 P+3 X-3 Q+2   E-2 G+1 S-1 F+3 U-2 P+4

＿＿＿＿ you ＿＿＿. ＿＿＿＿.
W+0 J-1 R+2 G+1     B-1 K+1 M-1.   D-3 O-2 F-1 L+2.

A B C D E F G H I J K L M N O P Q R S T U V W X Y Z

91

# Special Days

Christmas
Good Friday
Easter
Ascension
Pentecost
Christ's Second Coming
Valentine's Day
Mother's Day
Thanksgiving

# 81. Missing Objects

There are ten things left out of the second picture. Can you find them?

# 82. Star Maze

Help the wise men get through the maze to the young child, Jesus.

# 83. How to Draw Stars

How to make a star.

In the picture below, fill the sky with stars. Then color the picture.

# 84. How to Draw Sheep

The night Jesus was born, there were shepherds taking care of their sheep in the fields near Bethlehem.

You can draw a sheep by following the instructions below.

Pressing lightly with your pencil, draw a rectangle.

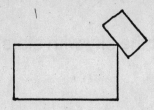

Add another as shown.

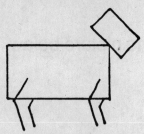

Make legs.

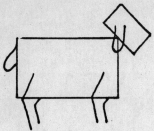

Add a tail and an ear.

Draw your sheep here.

Add wool as shown.

Add facial features and hooves; then erase unnecessary lines.

# 85. Make Your Own Picture

Using what you have learned on the page before, draw some sheep in the field below.

GLORY TO GOD IN THE HIGHEST!

# 86. Things in a Stable

Circle the items that could have been in the stable where Jesus was born.

# 87. The Angel's Message

Circle all the words of Luke 2:10 in this puzzle.

```
      O Y P U
    E E F E A R
    B U T O L D
    R O I P Y M
  S A I D R L O A I S
  T P N J B E U N T O
  A T G O O D S W E N
  T H E Y K S I A E M
  H A D I N G S N L L
  T E T R F O R R G L U S
  V M H A L L E U E I K T
  A D I A R F A F L W E U
  N O G O N O T C I E H T
```

"But the angel said to them, 'Do not be afraid. I bring you good news of great joy that will be for all the people.'"

# 88. Luke 19:10

Put the words in the right order to form Luke 19:10.

_____ _____ _____ _____ _____ _____ _____

_____ _____ _____ _____ _____ _____ _____.

# 89. Christmas Basket

Color the basket and handle and cut out on solid lines. Fold handle lengthwise on the dotted line, with holly leaves on the outside, and glue together. Form the basket into a cone and paste or tape. Attach the handle. Fill with small candy or other goodies and hang on the Christmas tree.

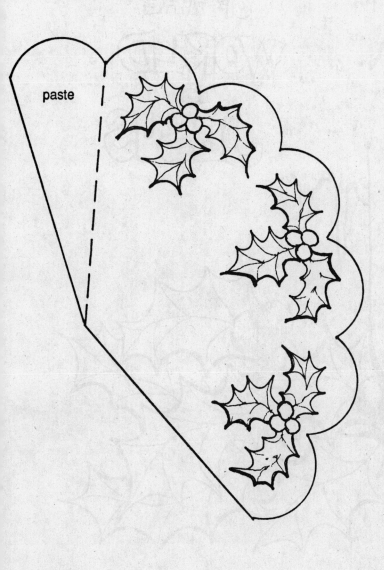

paste

# 90. Christmas Lights

THE LIGHT OF THE WORLD IS JESUS

# 91. The Angel's Message

Connect the dots to see what the angel told the shepherds; then color the picture.

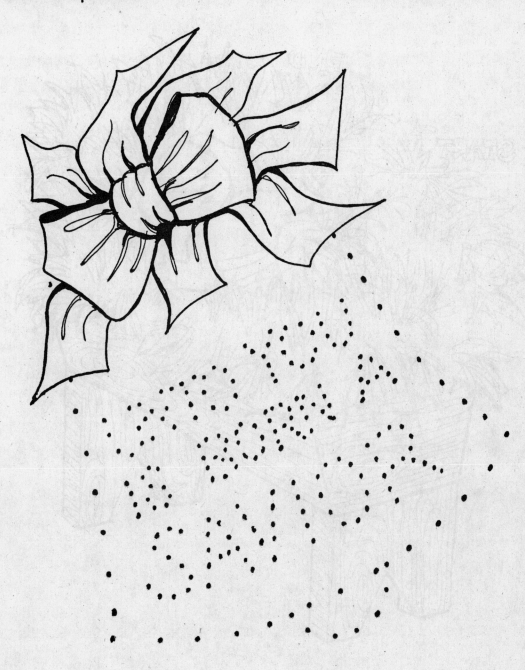

# 92. Straw Maze

Find your way through the straw maze. What is the baby's name?

_____  _  _____  _____  _____

# 93. Hidden Pictures

Find 3 stars, 2 bells, 1 angel, 3 crosses, 1 staff, and 2 candles hidden in the manger.

# 94. The Gift of God's Love

Find the answer to the following question by using the code in the letters on the present.

God's love was shown to us by sending

___ ___ ___ ___ ___
 D    O    V    E    S

# 95. The Reason for Christmas

Trace over the letters and color the picture.

# 96. Christmas Promise

*For to us a child is born, to us a Son is given*

*Isaiah 9:6*

Trace the letters and color the picture.

# 97. Christmas Doubles

Circle two pictures in each row that are the same.

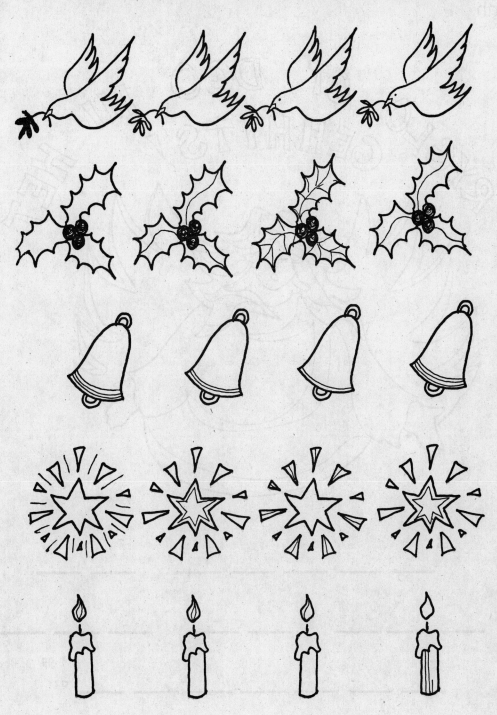

# 98. Angels' Message

Unscramble the words to find out what the angels said at Christ's birth.

"

__ __ __ __ __ __   __ __ __

__ __ __ __ __ __   __ __ __ __

"

__ __ __ __ __ __ __ __ __ __.

# 99. Christmas Wreath

Color the picture using the following code.

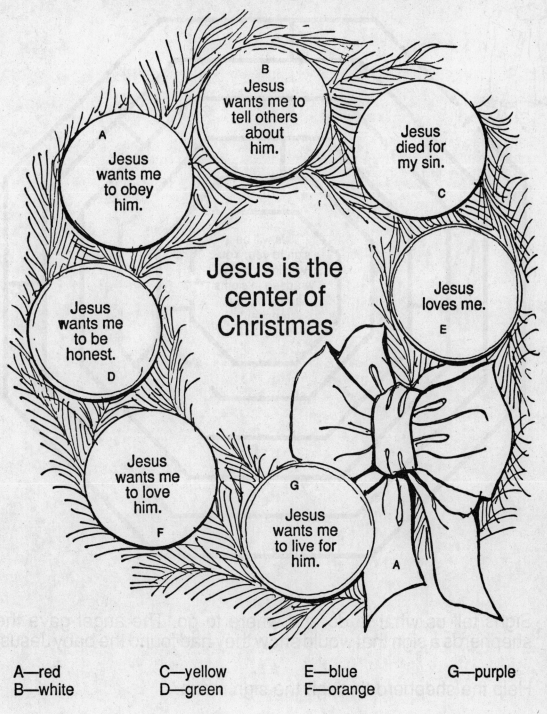

A
Jesus wants me to obey him.

B
Jesus wants me to tell others about him.

Jesus died for my sin.
C

Jesus wants me to be honest.
D

Jesus is the center of Christmas

Jesus loves me.
E

Jesus wants me to love him.
F

G
Jesus wants me to live for him.

A

A—red        C—yellow      E—blue        G—purple
B—white      D—green       F—orange

# 100. Sign Maze

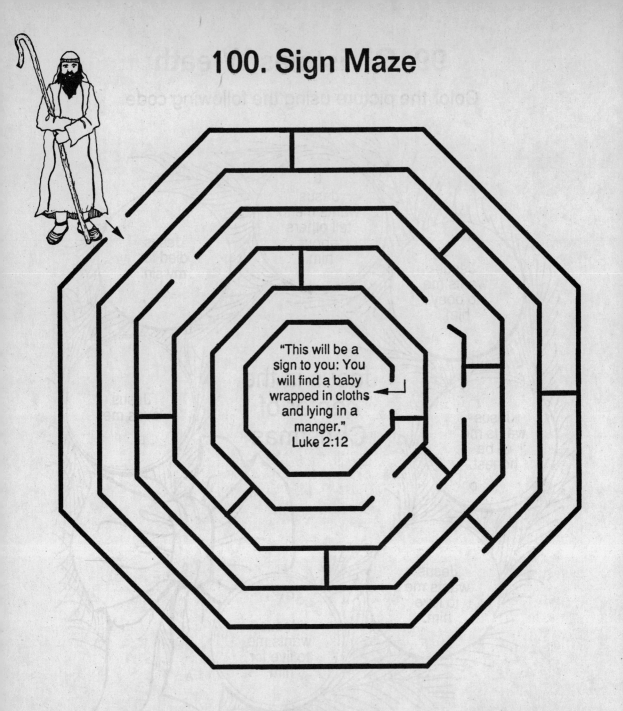

"This will be a sign to you: You will find a baby wrapped in cloths and lying in a manger."
Luke 2:12

Signs tell us what to do and where to go. The angel gave the shepherds a sign that would show they had found the baby Jesus.

Help the shepherd through the sign maze.

# 101. Jesus' Age When He Died

Add the numbers in the picture to find out how old Jesus was when he died on the cross. Then color the picture.

Do your figuring here.

# 102. Crown of Thorns Maze

Use a crayon or pencil to find your way through the crown of thorns.

START

FINISH

"The soldiers twisted together a crown of thorns, and put it on his head."

John 19:2

# 103. For Whom Did Jesus Die?

Jesus died for many kinds of people. Circle those you can find in the picture (there are 24); then write them down on the lines below.

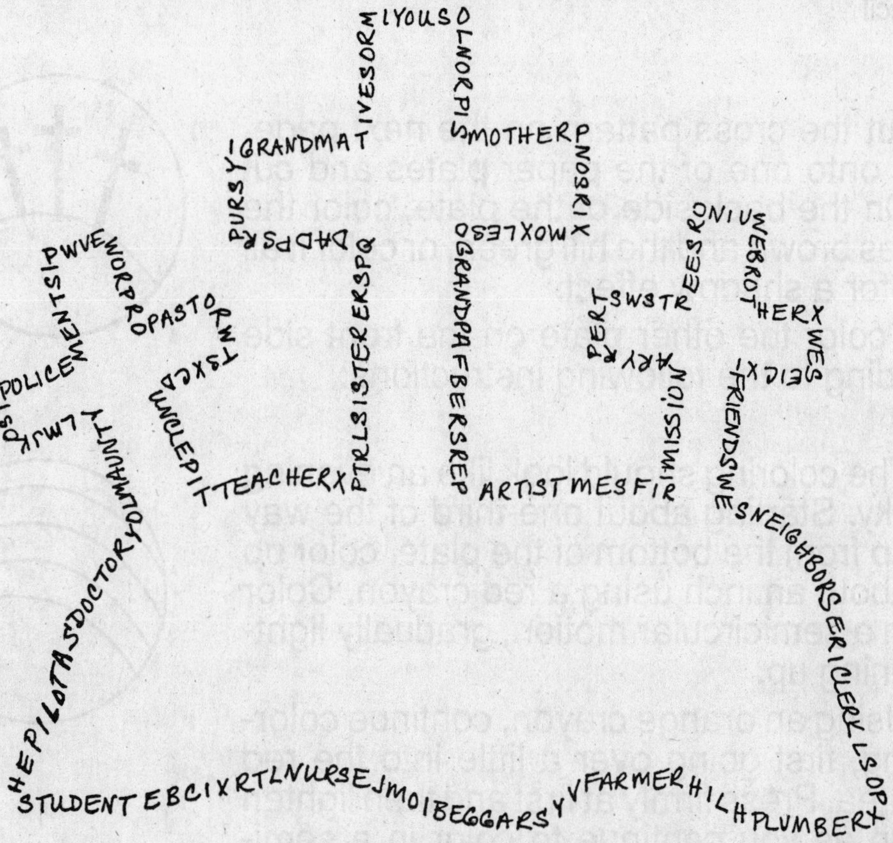

LYOUSO

OLNORPIS MOTHERP

IGRANDMAT IVESORM PNOSRIX

PURSY MWOXLES O

DADPSR Q

WORPRO OGRANDRAFBERSKEP WEBROT HERX

PWVE PASTO R OPOST POLICEMENTSI R WI TSXCD ARY X DICX

HEPILOTASDOCTORYOLWINTY UNCLEPIT TTEACHERX PTRLSISTER EKSPQ ARTISTMESFIR MISSION FRIENDSWE NEIGHBORSERICLERKLSOPX

STUDENT EBCIXRTLNURSEJMOIBEGGARSYVFARMER HILH PLUMBERX

---
(24 blank answer lines in three columns)

117

# 104. Paper Plate Crosses

Materials:
    two 9" paper plates          crayons
    scissors                     glue or stapler
    pencil

Cut out the cross pattern on the next page. Trace onto one of the paper plates and cut out. On the back side of the plate, color the crosses brown and the hill green, or color it all black for a shadow effect.

Next, color the other plate on the front side according to the following instructions:

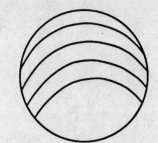

1.  The coloring should look like an evening sky. Starting about one-third of the way up from the bottom of the plate, color up about an inch using a red crayon. Color in a semicircular motion, gradually lightening up.

2.  Using an orange crayon, continue coloring, first going over a little into the red area. Press firmly at first and then lighten up as you continue to color in a semicircular motion about an inch.

3.  Using a yellow crayon, repeat step 2, ending by coloring very lightly.

4.  Finish coloring the plate with your blue crayon, using a light blue and then gradually pressing heavily around the top rim of the plate.

Glue or staple the rims of the plates together, the three crosses in front of the sky scene.

Fold an 8 1/2 x 11
sheet of paper in half.
Place the dotted edge
of the pattern on the
folded edge of the
paper. Staple the top,
bottom, and outside
edges. Cut along the
solid lines, unfold the
paper to reveal the full
pattern.

# 105. Christ Is Risen

*He Is Risen*

# 106. Easter Look-Alikes

Circle the two look-alikes in each row.

# 107. Easter Window

Color each shape with a number in it according to the key below.

1-green          3-red          5-purple
2-brown          4-blue         6-yellow

# 108. Mark 6:1–8

Hidden in the puzzle below are words from Mark 16:1–8, where we read the story of Jesus rising from the grave. Try to find all the words listed at the bottom of the page.

```
            L O F T O T R
        C B A S Z O S P I C E S
        T N I O N A T A G F C C
      P Q A Z D R A H X D H E S D
      K S U N R I S E F G T B S U
    S B E A B P T U W L E K R O L L E D
    T F E S A B B A T H R S T R S C V W
    O B W A T Q D E L F A B M O T F N L
    N T K S C M A R Y H
    E C R U C I F I E D
    M H I R Q P I O O A
    J E S U S S R S T Y
    Z V E T I U S V O P
    W Q N U A C T R X S
```

| | | |
|---|---|---|
| SABBATH | TOMB | CRUCIFIED |
| SPICES | STONE | RISEN |
| ANOINT | ROLLED | LAID |
| FIRST | RIGHT | FLED |
| DAY | ROBE | WEEK |
| SUNRISE | JESUS | MARY |

# 109. Angel at the Tomb

To find out what the angel said to the women at the tomb, unscramble the words in the opening.

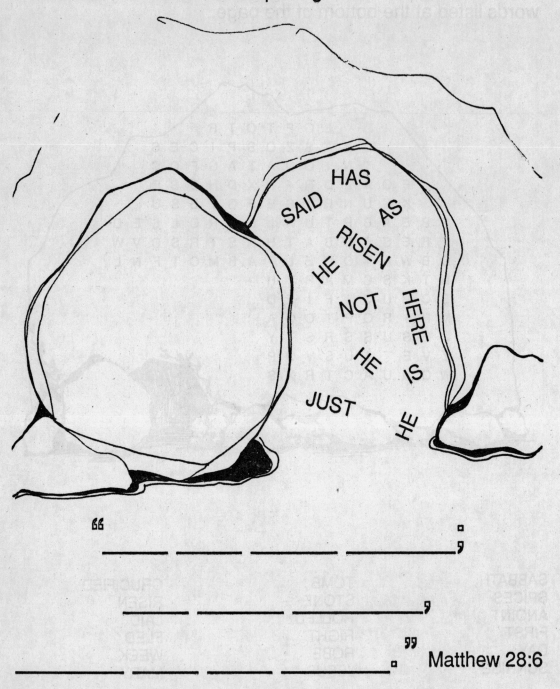

SAID HAS AS HE RISEN NOT HERE HE IS JUST HE

" _____ _____ _____ _____,

_____ _____ _____,

_____ _____ _____ _____. " Matthew 28:6

# 110. Easter Joy

Trace over the dotted lines and color the picture.

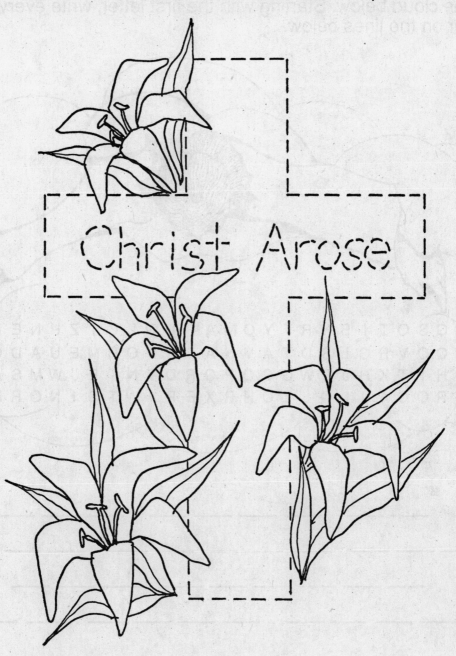

# 111. Jesus Said . . .

What did Jesus say before he returned to heaven? The answer is in the cloud below. Starting with the first letter, write every other letter on the lines below.

```
G S O T I B N R T Y O M A P L W L C T Z H N E L W
Q O V R G L S D T A V N A D W P Q R M E U A D C X
H I T K H J E W G S O P O R D V N T E J W M S A T
R O C A J L Q L Z C H R X E P A W T S I N O R N
```

" __ __ __ __ __ __ __ __ __ __ __ __

__ __ __ __ __ __ __ __ __ __ __ __ __

__ __ __ __ __ __ __ __ __ __ __ __

__ __ __ __ __ __ __ __ __ __ __

__ __ __ __ __ __ __ __ __ __ __ __ __ ."

Mark 16:15

126

# 112. What Happened at Pentecost?

Count the number of dots in each space. Then use the letters to decode the message below about what happened at Pentecost. Check your work with Acts 2:4.

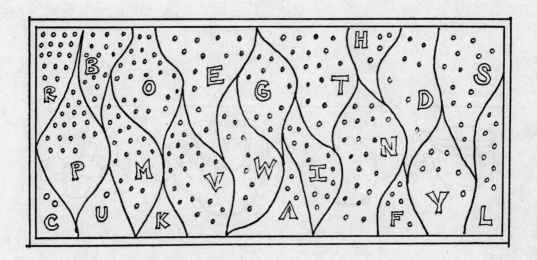

"

$\overline{3}\ \overline{8}\ \overline{8}$   $\overline{21}\ \overline{5}$   $\overline{15}\ \overline{4}\ \overline{12}\ \overline{16}$   $\overline{9}\ \overline{12}\ \overline{17}\ \overline{12}$   $\overline{5}\ \overline{11}\ \overline{8}\ \overline{8}\ \overline{12}\ \overline{7}$

$\overline{9}\ \overline{11}\ \overline{15}\ \overline{4}$   $\overline{15}\ \overline{4}\ \overline{12}$   $\overline{4}\ \overline{21}\ \overline{8}\ \overline{6}$   $\overline{13}\ \overline{18}\ \overline{11}\ \overline{17}\ \overline{11}\ \overline{15}$   $\overline{3}\ \overline{19}\ \overline{7}$

$\overline{14}\ \overline{12}\ \overline{10}\ \overline{3}\ \overline{19}$   $\overline{15}\ \overline{21}$   $\overline{13}\ \overline{18}\ \overline{12}\ \overline{3}\ \overline{0}$   $\overline{11}\ \overline{19}$   $\overline{21}\ \overline{15}\ \overline{4}\ \overline{12}\ \overline{17}$

$\overline{15}\ \overline{21}\ \overline{19}\ \overline{10}\ \overline{1}\ \overline{12}\ \overline{13}$   $\overline{3}\ \overline{13}$   $\overline{15}\ \overline{4}\ \overline{12}$   $\overline{13}\ \overline{18}\ \overline{11}\ \overline{17}\ \overline{11}\ \overline{15}$

$\overline{12}\ \overline{19}\ \overline{3}\ \overline{14}\ \overline{8}\ \overline{12}\ \overline{7}$   $\overline{15}\ \overline{4}\ \overline{12}\ \overline{16}$ ."

# 113. Jesus' Promise

Jesus made a promise before he went back to heaven. To find out what it was, fill in the blanks with the first letter of the picture below the line.

## Jesus promised he will

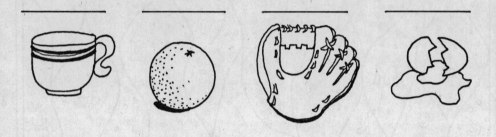

# 114. Jesus Is Coming Again

Connect the dots and then color the picture.

# 115. Christ's Return

Before Jesus went back to heaven, he told us to watch for his return. Matthew 24:36–46 tells about Christ's return. Some words from that passage are found in the puzzle below. Circle the words as you find them.

```
      A S F A
    S E R V A N T B
    O M E H I D H L
  A N A A O T W I H K
  U I N D U H I E A N
  P R A Y R F S F O O
  W A T C H U E O N W
  R O N Z L O R D
  K C O M I N G O
      E D A Y
```

| COMING | THIEF | UP | PRAY |
|--------|-------|-----|------|
| DAY | WATCH | DO | KNOW |
| SERVANT | ARK | LORD | FOR |
| MAN | HOUR | WISE | ON |
| IN | FAITHFUL | READY | |
| NOAH | SON | AN | |

# 116. A Promise

What did Jesus promise when he went back to heaven? To find the answer, write the first letter of the picture on the line above it.

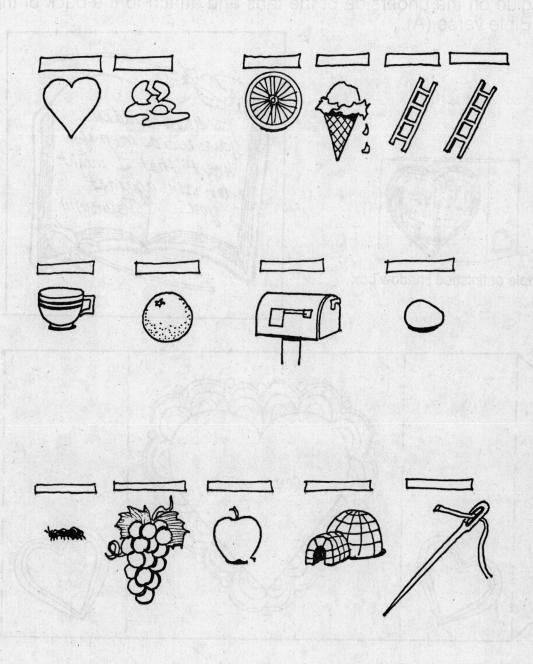

# 117. Valentine Shadow Box

Materials needed: crayons, glue, scissors

Color A and B. Cut out on solid lines. Fold on broken lines. Apply glue on the underside of the tabs and attach to the back of the Bible verse (A).

example of finished shadow box

A

*I have hidden your Word in my heart that I might not sin against you.* Psalm 119:11

B

(CUT OUT)

# 118. Love the Lord

Trace the words, then color the picture.

# 119. Count the Hearts

How many hearts can you find in the picture below?

I found_____ hearts.
Color the picture.

# 120. Heart Wreath

Use the code at the bottom of the page to fill in the blanks in the heart wreath. Then on each heart write a way that you can be friendly to others.

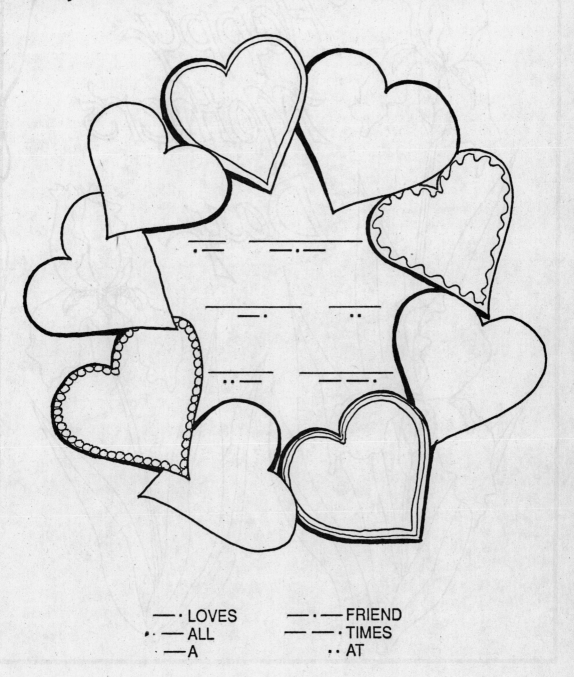

— · LOVES     — · — FRIEND
· · — ALL      — — · TIMES
— A        · · AT

# 121. Mother's Day Picture to Color

# 122. Thanksgiving

"Let us come before him with thanksgiving."
Psalm 95:2 (NIV)

How many words can you make using the letters in the word "THANKSGIVING"? Only use the letters as many times as shown.

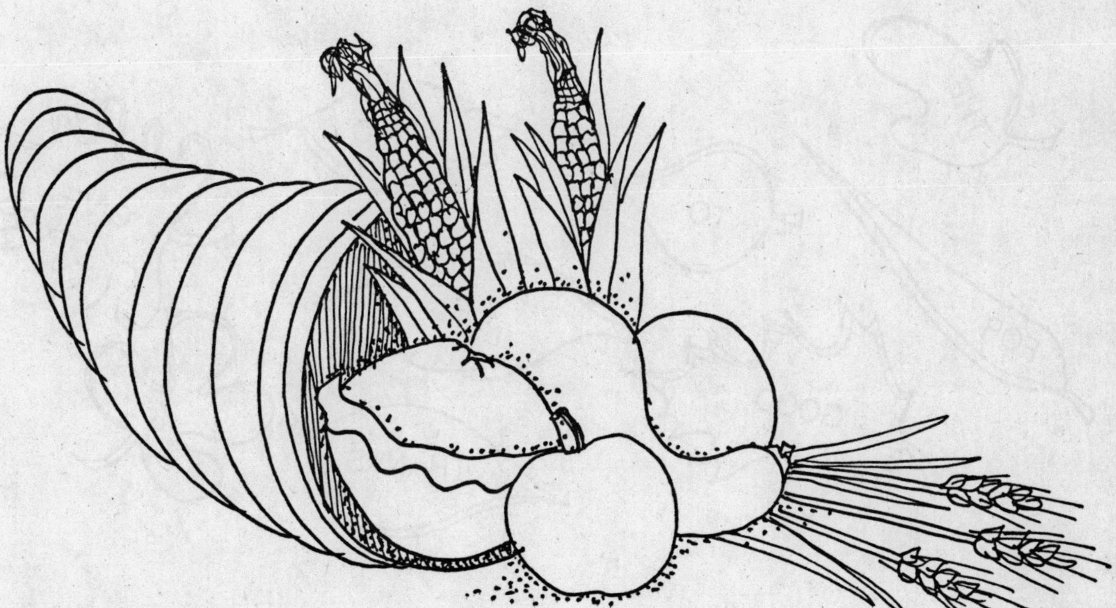

_____

_____

_____

_____

_____

_____

_____

_____

# 123. Psalm 107:1

On the line below each leaf write the word that appears in the matching leaf at the top of the page.

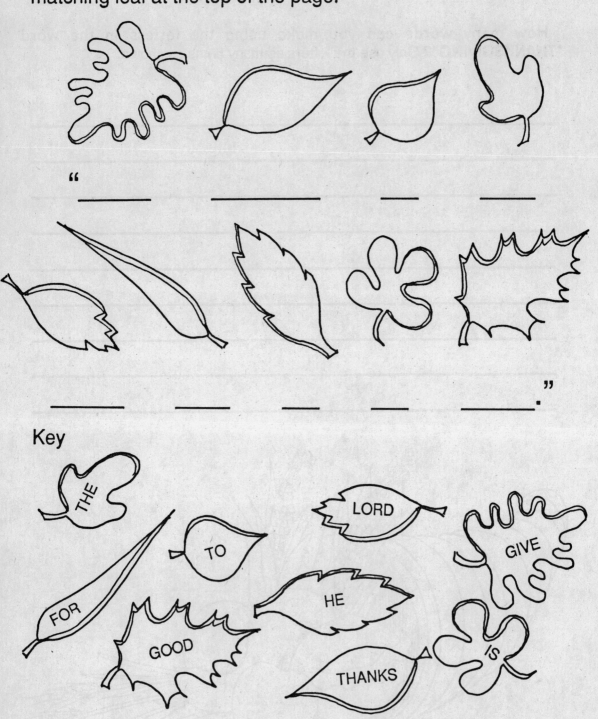

Key

# 124. Dinner Word Scramble

Often we celebrate Thanksgiving Day with friends and relatives by having a big dinner. Unscramble the words in the dishes and write them on the lines below.

_____     _____

_____     _____

_____     _____

_____     _____

# 125. Thanksgiving Word Scramble

We have many things to be thankful for. Unscramble the letters in the apples to find out what some of them are. Write the words on the lines below the basket.

_____     _____     _____
_____     _____     _____
_____     _____     _____

# Miscellaneous

# 126. The Holy Bible

The Holy Bible is the true word of God.

Solve the coded puzzle to find out how we know the Bible is true.

$$\overline{\alpha}\overline{\lambda}\overline{\lambda} \quad \overline{\sigma}\overline{\chi}\overline{\ast}\overline{\iota}\overline{\pi}\overline{\tau}\overline{\upsilon}\overline{\ast}\overline{\varepsilon} \quad \overline{\iota}\overline{\sigma}$$

$$\overline{\Gamma}\overline{\iota}\overline{\varphi}\overline{\varepsilon}\overline{\nu} \quad \overline{\beta}\overline{\psi} \quad \overline{\iota}\overline{\nu}\overline{\sigma}\overline{\pi}\overline{\iota}\overline{\ast}\overline{\alpha}\overline{\tau}\overline{\iota}\overline{\nu}$$

$$\overline{o}\overline{\phi} \quad \overline{\Gamma}\overline{o}\overline{\Delta}.$$ 2 Timothy 3:16

| A | B | C | D | E | F | G | H | I | J | L | N | O | P | R | S | T | U | V | Y |
|---|---|---|---|---|---|---|---|---|---|---|---|---|---|---|---|---|---|---|---|
| α | β | χ | Δ | ε | φ | Γ | η | ι | § | λ | ν | ο | π | ※ | σ | τ | υ | ϙ | ψ |

The Bible tells us about _____.
§εσυσ

God wants us to ____ ___ _____ every day.
※εαΔ τηε βιβλε

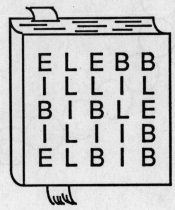

ELEBB
ILLIL
BIBLE
ILIIB
ELBIB

How many times can you find the word "BIBLE" in these letters?

# 127. Name Chain 1

Use the clues to fill in the name chain. The last letter of the first name will be the first letter of the second name and so on.

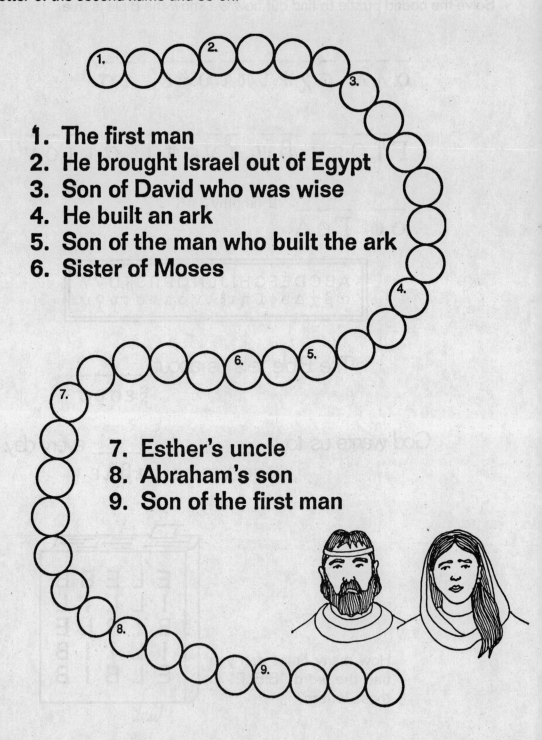

1. The first man
2. He brought Israel out of Egypt
3. Son of David who was wise
4. He built an ark
5. Son of the man who built the ark
6. Sister of Moses

7. Esther's uncle
8. Abraham's son
9. Son of the first man

# 128. Name Chain 2

Use the clues to fill in the name chain. The last letter of the first name will be the first letter of the second name and so on.

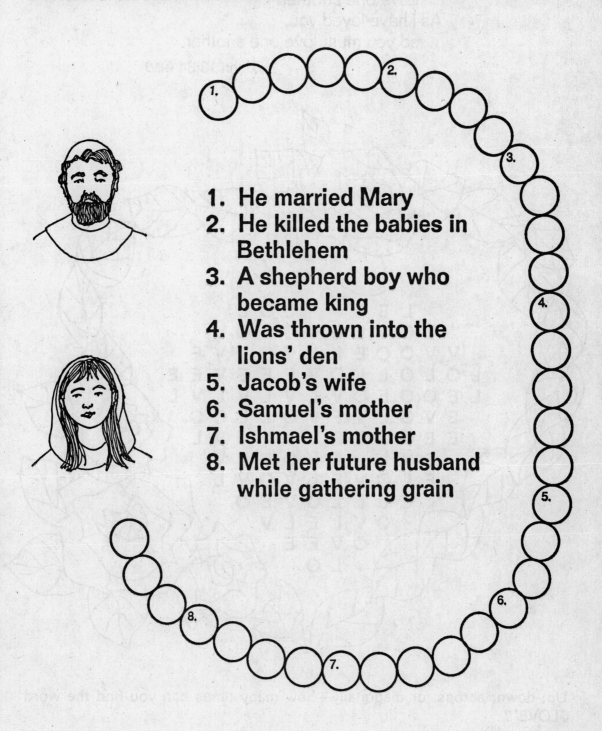

1. He married Mary
2. He killed the babies in Bethlehem
3. A shepherd boy who became king
4. Was thrown into the lions' den
5. Jacob's wife
6. Samuel's mother
7. Ishmael's mother
8. Met her future husband while gathering grain

# 129. Love

A new commandment I give you:
Love one another.
As I have loved you,
   so you must love one another.

John 13:34 (NIV)

```
    L E E       L O L
   L O V E E   V O L O V
  V V O O E L L V O V V E
 L O L O L L O V E E E V E E
 L E O O E O V L V L V L V L
  E V O L V E V O L L O O
  E E O O E O V L V V V L
   E V L L E L O E E V
   E L O V E L V O V L
    E L L L O V E O
    O V L E L V
     O V E E
      L O
```

Up, down, across, or diagonally—how many times can you find the word "LOVE"?

146

# 130. Prayer

Use the American Manual Alphabet to solve the puzzle on prayer.

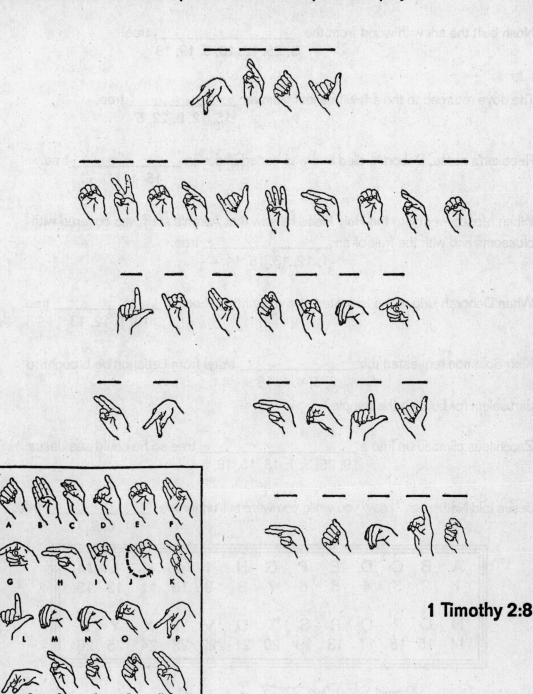

**1 Timothy 2:8**

# 131. Trees in the Bible

Use the code below to find the names of the trees in each sentence.

Noah built the ark with wood from the _____ tree.
3, 25, 16, 18, 5, 19, 19

The dove returned to the ark with a leaf from an _____ tree.
15, 12, 9, 22, 5

Rebekah's nurse, Deborah, died and was buried under an _____ tree.
15, 1, 11

When Moses went into the Holy Place he saw that Aaron's staff was covered with blossoms and with the fruit of an _____ tree.
1, 12, 13, 15, 14, 4

When Deborah judged the Israelites she was sitting under a _____ tree.
16, 1, 12, 13

King Solomon requested that _____ trees from Lebanon be brought to
3, 5, 4, 1, 18

Jerusalem for building the temple.

Zacchaeus climbed up into a _____ tree so he could see Jesus.
19, 25, 3, 1, 13, 15, 18, 5

Jesus told Nathanael, "I saw you while you were still under the _____ tree."
6, 9, 7

| A | B | C | D | E | F | G | H | I | J | K | L | M |
|---|---|---|---|---|---|---|---|---|---|---|---|---|
| 1 | 2 | 3 | 4 | 5 | 6 | 7 | 8 | 9 | 10 | 11 | 12 | 13 |

| N | O | P | Q | R | S | T | U | V | W | X | Y | Z |
|---|---|---|---|---|---|---|---|---|---|---|---|---|
| 14 | 15 | 16 | 17 | 18 | 19 | 20 | 21 | 22 | 23 | 24 | 25 | 26 |

# 132. Clouds

Try to guess the name of the person in each story. If you don't know the answer, look in your Bible.

Moses led the Israelites out of Egypt, and _____ went ahead of them in a pillar of cloud. Exodus 13:21

After a long drought, _____ prayed for rain, and his servant said that a cloud as small as a man's hand was rising from the sea. 1 Kings 18:42–44

_____, _____, and _____ were on the mountain with Jesus when _____ and Elijah appeared. Then a bright cloud came over them and a voice said, "This is my beloved Son, in whom I am well pleased; hear ye him." Matthew 17:3–5

When _____ ascended to heaven a cloud hid him from the disciples' sight. Acts 1:9–11

_____ said he would return in the clouds of heaven with power and great glory. Matthew 24:30

Some other Bible verses about clouds are: Psalm 104:3; Proverbs 16:15; Isaiah 19:1; 1 Thessalonians 4:17; Revelation 1:7; 14:14

Unscramble the names of the different types of clouds below.

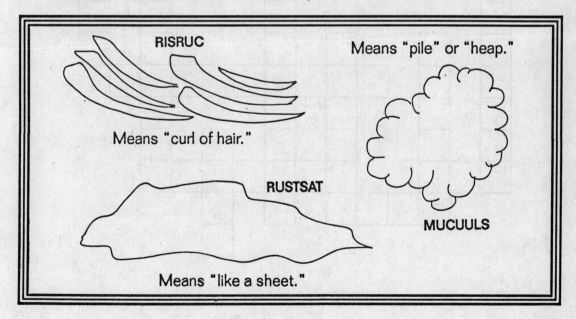

RISRUC
Means "pile" or "heap."
Means "curl of hair."
RUSTSAT
MUCUULS
Means "like a sheet."

# 133. Mothers

Try to do the crossword puzzle without using the wiggly lines. Name the mother of each of the children in the left-hand column.

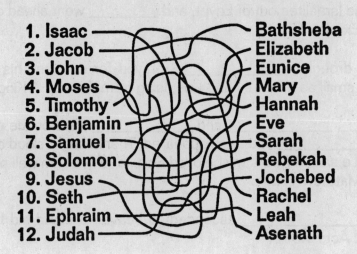

1. Isaac
2. Jacob
3. John
4. Moses
5. Timothy
6. Benjamin
7. Samuel
8. Solomon
9. Jesus
10. Seth
11. Ephraim
12. Judah

Bathsheba
Elizabeth
Eunice
Mary
Hannah
Eve
Sarah
Rebekah
Jochebed
Rachel
Leah
Asenath

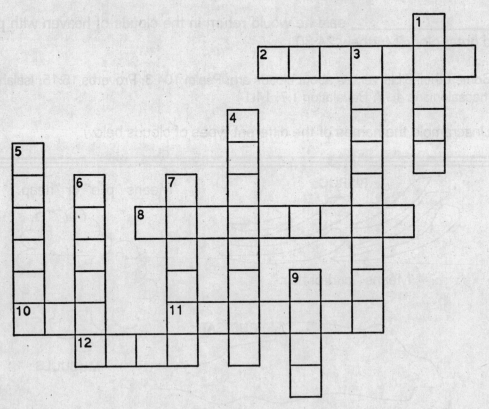

# 134. Sisters

Follow the line from the man's name on the left to find his sister.

Laban   Dinah

Judah   Miriam

Absalom   Rebekah

Moses   Tamar

Agrippa   Bernice

Now fit the sisters' names in the puzzle.

| S | I | S | T | E | R | S |
|---|---|---|---|---|---|---|

# ANSWERS

## 1. CREATION
ODD, DAY, DAYS, SEE, SEED, EDEN, DEN, DENS, DENSE, SEA, SEAS, SEASON, SEASONS, AS, SON, SONS, ON, FOWL, OWL, LAIR, AIR, BE, BEAST, EAST

## 2. THE GARDEN OF EDEN
THE TREE OF LIFE
THE TREE OF KNOWLEDGE OF GOOD AND EVIL
THE TREE OF KNOWLEDGE OF GOOD AND EVIL

## 4. LOT'S CHOICE
LOT CHOSE THE PLAIN OF JORDAN AND PITCHED HIS TENT NEAR SODOM. THE MEN OF SODOM WERE WICKED.

## 5. ABRAHAM AND ISAAC WORSHIP ON THE MOUNTAIN
GOD SAID "NOW I KNOW THAT YOU FEAR GOD." GOD HIMSELF WILL PROVIDE THE LAMB.

## 6. STAIRWAY TO HEAVEN
JOURNEY, TIRED, STONE, DREAM, ANGELS, GOD, BLESSED, OIL, PROMISE, BETHEL

## 7. SONS OF JACOB

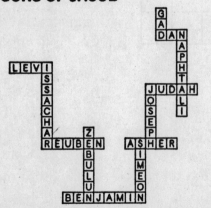

## 8. WILDERNESS MENU
1. OMER
2. FORTY YEARS
3. BREAD FROM HEAVEN
4. HONEY
5. QUAIL

## 9. THE GOLDEN CALF
MOSES THREW DOWN THE STONE TABLETS OF THE TEN COMMANDMENTS.
HE GROUND THE CALF INTO POWDER AND THREW IT INTO THE DRINKING WATER.

## 10. THE CLUSTER OF GRAPES
THE PEOPLE ARE GIANTS AND WE FELT LIKE GRASSHOPPERS BESIDE THEM.

## 11. A TALKING DONKEY
GO TO BALAK BUT ONLY SAY WHAT GOD GIVES YOU TO SPEAK.

## 12. RAHAB

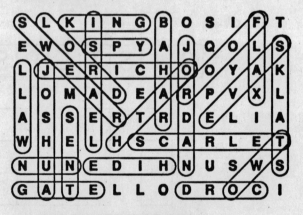

## 14. THE SUN STANDS STILL
AND THE SUN STOOD STILL AND THE MOON STAYED UNTIL THE PEOPLE HAD AVENGED THEMSELVES UPON THEIR ENEMIES.

## 15. DEBORAH
JUDGE
SISERA
BARAK
SONG
DRINK
JAEL
PROPHETESS

## 16. GIDEON

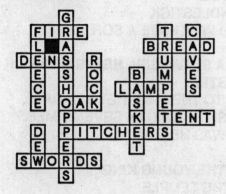

## 17. RUTH

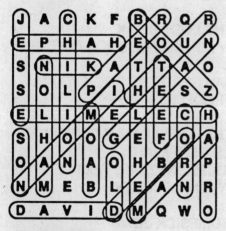

## 18. SAMUEL
EBENEZER

## 19. THE FIRST KING
ISRAEL
SAMUEL
ISRAELITE
BENJAMIN

KISH
SAUL

## 20. THE BRAVE YOUNG PRINCE

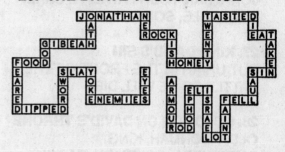

## 21. THE SHEPHERD BOY OF BETHLEHEM
MAN LOOKS AT THE OUTWARD APPEARANCE BUT THE LORD LOOKS AT THE HEART.
DAVID

## 22. DAVID AND GOLIATH
SWORDS, WORD, WORDS, OR, STONE, STONES, TON, TONE, TONES, ONE, ON, NEST, TENT, TENTS, TEN, SLING, LINGO, IN, GO, GOD, DOG, DO, GIANT, ANT, AN

## 23. JONATHAN'S SECRET CODE
THAT THERE WAS PEACE.
GO AWAY, MY FATHER WANTS TO KILL YOU.

## 24. PSALM 100

153

### 26. A LAME BOY AT THE KING'S TABLE
I WILL SHOW YOU KINDNESS FOR JONATHAN YOUR FATHER'S SAKE. EAT, TABLE, SONS

### 27. KING DAVID'S SIN
PUT URIAH IN THE FRONT OF THE BATTLE SO HE WILL DIE.

### 28. SOLOMON ON DAVID'S THRONE
OLD, ADONIJAH, KING, BATHSHEBA, SOLOMON, ZADOK, NATHAN, MULE, ANOINT, OIL, TRUMPET, GOD SAVE KING SOLOMON, AFRAID, HORNS, ALTAR, MERCY

### 29. ELIJAH

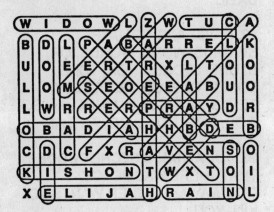

### 30. AN ENEMY AND A FRIEND
ELISHA
LORD
IDOL
JEZEBEL
AHAB
HUNGRY

### 31. ELIJAH'S DEPARTURE
LET ME INHERIT A DOUBLE PORTION OF YOUR SPIRIT.

A CHARIOT AND HORSES OF FIRE CAME AND TOOK HIM IN A WHIRLWIND.

### 33. THE WOMAN OF SHUNEM
BREAD
CHAMBER
BED
TABLE
STOOL
CANDLESTICK
YOU WILL HAVE A SON.

### 34. A SLAVE GIRL HELPS HER SICK MASTER
GO TO THE PROPHET IN ISRAEL. WASH IN JORDAN SEVEN TIMES. HE WAS HEALED.

### 35. THE YOUNG KING
IN THE TEMPLE
SEVEN
FIX THE TEMPLE

### 36. THE LOST BOOK
THEY FOUND THE BOOK OF THE LAW.
JOSIAH READ THE BOOK TO ALL THE PEOPLE.

### 37. THE BABYLONIAN CAPTIVITY
IDOLS, JEREMIAH, NEBUCHADNEZZAR, TEMPLE, BABYLON, SEVENTY

### 38. HOMESICK JEWS

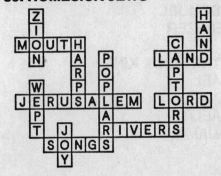

## 39. THE HAND THAT WROTE ON THE WALL
HE DID NOT HONOR GOD

## 40. RETURN TO ZION

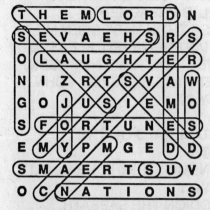

## 41. PROPHETS PREDICT BABY'S BIRTH
FOR UNTO US A CHILD IS BORN.
CALL HIS NAME IMMANUEL.
BEHOLD THY KING COMETH.
BETHLEHEM . . . OUT OF THEE
SHALL HE COME.

## 42. JOSEPH'S DREAM
FEAR NOT TO TAKE UNTO THEE
MARY AS THY WIFE, FOR THAT
WHICH IS CONCEIVED IN HER IS OF
THE HOLY SPIRIT.

## 43. AND HIS NAME SHALL BE CALLED . . .

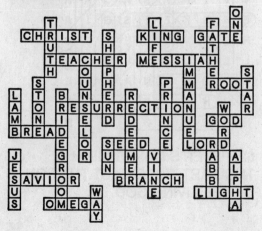

## 44. WISE MEN WORSHIP JESUS
STAR
HEROD
JOY

## 45. JOHN THE BAPTIST
BEHOLD THE LAMB OF GOD WHO
TAKES AWAY THE SIN OF THE
WORLD.
REPENT FOR THE KINGDOM OF
HEAVEN IS AT HAND.

## 46. FISHERS OF MEN
PETER—HIS NAME MEANS "ROCK"
ANDREW—PETER'S BROTHER
JAMES—BROTHER OF JOHN
JOHN—SON OF ZEBEDEE AND
BROTHER OF JAMES
PHILIP—HE BROUGHT NATHANAEL
TO JESUS
MATTHEW—A TAX COLLECTOR
THOMAS—ALSO CALLED DIDYMUS
JAMES—SON OF ALPHAEUS (ALSO
CALLED "THE LESS")
SIMON—A CANAANITE, ALSO
CALLED ZELOTES
JUDAS—BETRAYED JESUS
BARTHOLOMEW, THADDAEUS

## 47. THE BEATITUDES

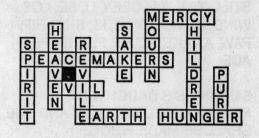

## 48. SERMON ON THE MOUNT
NO MAN CAN SERVE TWO
MASTERS

## 49. THE GOOD SAMARITAN

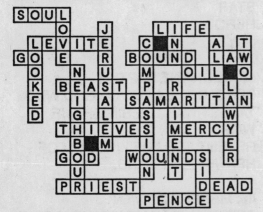

## 50. THE FOOLISH RICH MAN
LAY NOT UP FOR YOURSELVES TREASURES UPON EARTH; . . . LAY UP FOR YOURSELVES TREASURES IN HEAVEN. . . . FOR WHERE YOUR TREASURE IS, THERE WILL YOUR HEART BE ALSO.

## 51. MIDNIGHT VISITOR
YOUR FATHER WHICH IS IN HEAVEN WILL GIVE GOOD THINGS TO THEM THAT ASK HIM. MATTHEW 7:11

## 52. JESUS CALMS THE STORM
STORMS, OR, SEA, SEAS, AS, EAST, STILL, TILL, ILL, OBEY, LOBE, LOB, WIND, IN, WIN, DISH, IS, SHIP, HIP, PAW, AWAKE, WAKE, PEACE, PEA, ACE

## 54. JAIRUS'S DAUGHTER
FEAR NOT, BELIEVE ONLY AND SHE SHALL BE MADE WHOLE.

## 55. JESUS CHOOSES TWELVE DISCIPLES
1. SPENT THE NIGHT IN PRAYER
2. PREACH THE GOSPEL AND HEAL

## 56. JOHN'S QUESTION ANSWERED
THE BLIND SEE, THE LAME WALK, THE LEPERS ARE CLEANSED, THE DEAF HEAR, THE DEAD ARE RAISED, TO THE POOR THE GOSPEL IS PREACHED. BECAUSE THOU HAST SEEN ME, THOU HAST BELIEVED: BLESSED ARE THEY THAT HAVE NOT SEEN, AND YET HAVE BELIEVED. JOHN TWENTY 29.

## 57. JESUS HEALS ON THE SABBATH
MAN, ENEMIES, RIGHT, HEAL, OUT, NEW, AWAY
DO GOOD ON THE SABBATH.

## 60. PETER WALKS ON THE WATER
TRUST IN THE LORD WITH ALL THINE HEART AND LEAN NOT UNTO THINE OWN UNDERSTANDING. PROVERBS 3:5

## 61. JESUS FEEDS THE FIVE THOUSAND

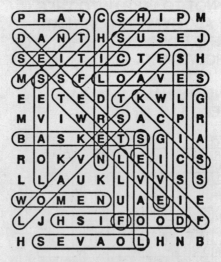

## 62. PETER'S CONFESSION
THOU ART THE CHRIST THE SON OF THE LIVING GOD.

### 63. JESUS' TRANSFIGURATION

THIS IS MY BELOVED SON IN WHOM I AM WELL PLEASED. HEAR YE HIM.

### 64. SEVENTY TIMES SEVEN

AS THE LORD HAS FORGIVEN YOU, SO YOU ALSO MUST FORGIVE.

### 65. THE UNFORGIVING SERVANT

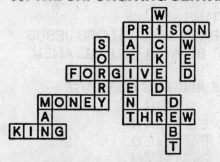

### 67. JESUS HEALS THE BLIND MAN

IN, DO, DOPE, PEA, PEACE, ACE, ACES, SON, SONS, ON, SAT, AT, BE, BEG, EGO, GOD, PRAISE, RAISE, IS, SEE, SEEM, MA, MAN, AN

### 68. THE PARABLE OF THE TWO SONS

I WILL NOT GO TO WORK.
HE WENT TO WORK.
I WILL GO TO WORK.
HE DIDN'T GO TO WORK.
IF YOU LOVE ME, YOU WILL OBEY ME.

### 69. THE GREATEST COMMANDMENT

THOU SHALT LOVE THE LORD THY GOD WITH ALL THY HEART, AND WITH ALL THY SOUL, AND WITH ALL THY MIND.
THOU SHALT LOVE THY NEIGHBOR AS THYSELF.

### 70. JESUS' SECOND COMING

BUT OF THAT DAY AND HOUR KNOWETH NO MAN, NO, NOT THE ANGELS OF HEAVEN, BUT MY FATHER ONLY.

### 71. A PARABLE

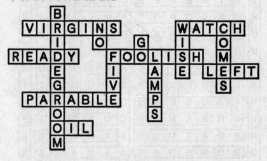

### 72. MARY ANOINTS JESUS' FEET

HOW BEAUTIFUL UPON THE MOUNTAINS ARE THE FEET OF HIM THAT BRINGS GOOD TIDINGS.

### 73. THE LAST SUPPER

| | |
|---|---|
| (5) PASSOVER | (4) DRINK |
| (1) BETRAY | (3) BLOOD |
| (6) BODY | (2) SHED |

### 74. PETER'S DENIAL

LORD, I WILL NOT DENY YOU.
AND AGAIN HE DENIED WITH AN OATH, I DO NOT KNOW THE MAN.

### 75. CHRIST DIED FOR OUR SINS

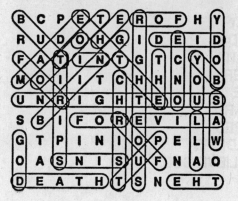

## 76. HE IS RISEN!
GOD RAISED HIM FROM THE DEAD.
ACTS 3:15 (NIV)

## 77. PENTECOST

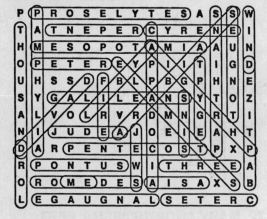

## 78. ANANIAS AND SAPPHIRA
SOME LAND
SOME OF THE MONEY
ALL OF THE MONEY
PETER
DIED
DID NOT KNOW
WANTED TO KNOW IF SHE WAS
    LYING
GOD

## 79. PAUL SHIPWRECKED
SHIP
BLEW
SEA
ITALY
WINDS
MELITA
VIPER
FIRE
GUARD
ROPES
SOLDIERS
I BELIEVE GOD.

## 80. LETTERS FROM A PRISONER
1 & 2 THESSALONIANS
1 & 2 CORINTHIANS
PHILIPPIANS
1 & 2 TIMOTHY
COLOSSIANS
EPHESIANS
ROMANS
PHILEMON
TITUS
GALATIANS
THE GRACE OF OUR LORD JESUS
CHRIST BE WITH YOU ALL. AMEN.

## 87. THE ANGEL'S MESSAGE

## 88. LUKE 19:10
FOR THE SON OF MAN CAME TO SEEK
AND TO SAVE WHAT WAS LOST. LUKE
19:10

## 94. THE GIFT OF GOD'S LOVE
JESUS

## 98. ANGELS' MESSAGE
GLORY TO GOD IN THE HIGHEST.

## 101. JESUS' AGE WHEN HE DIED
3 + 7 + 2 + 4 + 5 + 1 + 3 + 8 = 33

## 103. FOR WHOM DID JESUS DIE?

PILOT
DOCTOR
AUNT
POLICEMEN
PASTOR
UNCLE
TEACHER
SISTER
DAD

GRANDMA
YOU
MOTHER
GRANDPA
ARTIST
MISSIONARY
BROTHER
FRIENDS
NEIGHBORS

CLERK
PLUMBER
FARMER
BEGGARS
NURSE
STUDENT

## 108. MARK 6:1–8

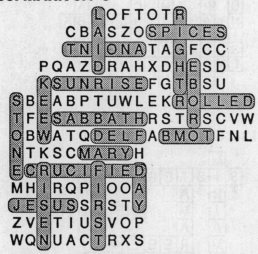

## 109. ANGEL AT THE TOMB

HE IS NOT HERE; HE HAS RISEN, JUST AS HE SAID.

## 111. JESUS SAID . . .

GO INTO ALL THE WORLD AND PREACH THE GOOD NEWS TO ALL CREATION.

## 112. WHAT HAPPENED AT PENTECOST?

ALL OF THEM WERE FILLED WITH THE HOLY SPIRIT AND BEGAN TO SPEAK IN OTHER TONGUES AS THE SPIRIT EN-ABLED THEM.

## 113. JESUS' PROMISE

COME AGAIN

## 115. CHRIST'S RETURN

## 116. A PROMISE

HE WILL COME AGAIN

## 119. COUNT THE HEARTS

67 hearts

## 120. HEART WREATH

A FRIEND LOVES AT ALL TIMES.

## 123. PSALM 107:1

GIVE THANKS TO THE LORD FOR HE IS GOOD.

## 124. DINNER WORD SCRAMBLE

TURKEY
CORN
POTATOES
BREAD
PIE

DRESSING
MILK
SALAD
BUTTER
PEAS

## 125. THANKSGIVING WORD SCRAMBLE

SCHOOL
HOME
FOOD
CLOTHES
CHURCH

FRIENDS
BIBLE
JESUS
PARENTS

## 126. THE HOLY BIBLE
ALL SCRIPTURE IS GIVEN BY
INSPIRATION OF GOD.
JESUS
READ THE BIBLE

## 127. NAME CHAIN 1
ADAM
MOSES
SOLOMON
NOAH
HAM

MIRIAM
MORDECAI
ISAAC
CAIN

## 128. NAME CHAIN 2
JOSEPH
HEROD
DAVID
DANIEL

LEAH
HANNAH
HAGAR
RUTH

## 130. PRAYER
PRAY EVERYWHERE, LIFTING UP
HOLY HANDS.

## 131. TREES IN THE BIBLE
CYPRESS
OLIVE
OAK
ALMOND

PALM
CEDAR
SYCAMORE
FIG

## 132. CLOUDS
GOD
ELIJAH
PETER
JAMES
JOHN

MOSES
JESUS
JESUS
CLOUDS = CIRRUS,
STRATUS, CUMULUS

## 133. MOTHERS

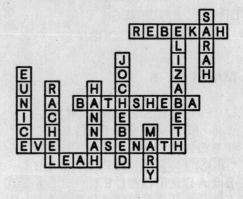

## 134. SISTERS

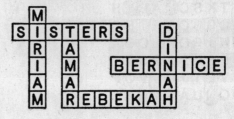